T0384932

An Analysis of

Benedict Anderson's

Imagined Communities

Jason Xidias

Published by Macat International Ltd
24:13 Coda Centre, 189 Munster Road, London SW6 6AW.

Distributed exclusively by Routledge
2 Park Square, Milton Park, Abingdon, Oxon OX14 4RN
711 Third Avenue, New York, NY 10017, USA

Routledge is an imprint of the Taylor & Francis Group, an informa business

www.macat.com
info@macat.com

Cataloguing in Publication Data
A catalogue record for this book is available from the British Library.
Library of Congress Cataloguing-in-Publication Data is available upon request.
Cover illustration: Etienne Gilfillan

ISBN 978-1-912303-16-8 (hardback)
ISBN 978-1-912127-01-6 (paperback)
ISBN 978-1-912282-04-3 (e-book)

Notice
The information in this book is designed to orientate readers of the work under analysis,
to elucidate and contextualise its key ideas and themes, and to aid in the development
of critical thinking skills. It is not meant to be used, nor should it be used, as a
substitute for original thinking or in place of original writing or research. References and
notes are provided for informational purposes and their presence does not constitute
endorsement of the information or opinions therein. This book is presented solely for
educational purposes. It is sold on the understanding that the publisher is not engaged
to provide any scholarly advice. The publisher has made every effort to ensure that
this book is accurate and up-to-date, but makes no warranties or representations with
regard to the completeness or reliability of the information it contains. The information
and the opinions provided herein are not guaranteed or warranted to produce particular
results and may not be suitable for students of every ability. The publisher shall not be
liable for any loss, damage or disruption arising from any errors or omissions, or from
the use of this book, including, but not limited to, special, incidental, consequential or
other damages caused, or alleged to have been caused, directly or indirectly, by the
information contained within.

CONTENTS

THE MACAT LIBRARY

The Macat Library is a series of unique academic explorations of seminal works in the humanities and social sciences – books and papers that have had a significant and widely recognised impact on their disciplines. It has been created to serve as much more than just a summary of what lies between the covers of a great book. It illuminates and explores the influences on, ideas of, and impact of that book. Our goal is to offer a learning resource that encourages critical thinking and fosters a better, deeper understanding of important ideas.

Each publication is divided into three Sections: Influences, Ideas, and Impact. Each Section has four Modules. These explore every important facet of the work, and the responses to it.

This Section-Module structure makes a Macat Library book easy to use, but it has another important feature. Because each Macat book is written to the same format, it is possible (and encouraged!) to cross-reference multiple Macat books along the same lines of inquiry or research. This allows the reader to open up interesting interdisciplinary pathways.

To further aid your reading, lists of glossary terms and people mentioned are included at the end of this book (these are indicated by an asterisk [*] throughout) – as well as a list of works cited.

Macat has worked with the University of Cambridge to identify the elements of critical thinking and understand the ways in which six different skills combine to enable effective thinking.
Three allow us to fully understand a problem; three more give us the tools to solve it. Together, these six skills make up the **PACIER** model of critical thinking. They are:

ANALYSIS – understanding how an argument is built
EVALUATION – exploring the strengths and weaknesses of an argument
INTERPRETATION – understanding issues of meaning

CREATIVE THINKING – coming up with new ideas and fresh connections
PROBLEM-SOLVING – producing strong solutions
REASONING – creating strong arguments

To find out more, visit **WWW.MACAT.COM.**

CRITICAL THINKING AND *IMAGINED COMMUNITIES*

Primary critical thinking skill: INTERPRETATION
Secondary critical thinking skill: ANALYSIS

Benedict Anderson's 1983 masterpiece *Imagined Communities* is a ground-breaking analysis of the origins and meanings of "nations" and "nationalism". A book that helped reshape the field of nationalism studies, *Imagined Communities* also shows the critical thinking skills of interpretation and analysis working at their highest levels. One crucial aspect of Anderson's work involves the apparently simple act of defining precisely what we mean when we say 'nation' or 'nationalism' – an interpretative step that is vital to the analysis he proceeds to carry out. For Anderson, it is clear that nations are not 'natural;' as historians and anthropologists are well aware, nations as we understand them are a relatively modern phenomenon, dating back only as far as around 1500. But if this is the case, how can we agree what a 'nation' is? Anderson's proposed definition is that they are "imagined communities" – comprising groups of people who regard themselves as belonging to the same community, even if they have never met, and have nothing in common otherwise. The analysis that follows from this insight is all about examining and breaking down the historical processes that helped foster these communities – above all the birth of printing, and the development of capitalism. Brilliantly incisive, Anderson's analysis shows how good interpretative skills can form the foundations for compelling and original insight.

ABOUT THE AUTHOR OF THE ORIGINAL WORK

Benedict Anderson was born on August 26, 1936, in Kunming, China, and lived in both California and Ireland as a child. He was of mixed Anglo-Irish heritage, and some of his family members were actively involved in Irish nationalist politics. Anderson was educated at the elite Eton College in England, and went on to study classics at Cambridge. As he started his postgraduate studies in the United States the mid-1960s, Anderson's personal background and the global unrest of the time that was caused by decolonization and ideological wars all influenced his decision to shift his focus to the study of nationalism. He ended his career as Professor Emeritus of International Studies at Cornell University in the United States, specializing in Southeast Asia, and died in 2015.

ABOUT THE AUTHOR OF THE ANALYSIS

Dr Jason Xidias holds a PhD in European Politics from King's College London, where he completed a comparative dissertation on immigration and citizenship in Britain and France. He was also a Visiting Fellow in European Politics at the University of California, Berkeley. Currently, he is Lecturer in Political Science at New York University.

ABOUT MACAT

GREAT WORKS FOR CRITICAL THINKING

Macat is focused on making the ideas of the world's great thinkers accessible and comprehensible to everybody, everywhere, in ways that promote the development of enhanced critical thinking skills.

It works with leading academics from the world's top universities to produce new analyses that focus on the ideas and the impact of the most influential works ever written across a wide variety of academic disciplines. Each of the works that sit at the heart of its growing library is an enduring example of great thinking. But by setting them in context – and looking at the influences that shaped their authors, as well as the responses they provoked – Macat encourages readers to look at these classics and game-changers with fresh eyes. Readers learn to think, engage and challenge their ideas, rather than simply accepting them.

'Macat offers an amazing first-of-its-kind tool for interdisciplinary learning and research. Its focus on works that transformed their disciplines and its rigorous approach, drawing on the world's leading experts and educational institutions, opens up a world-class education to anyone.'

Andreas Schleicher
Director for Education and Skills, Organisation for Economic Co-operation and Development

'Macat is taking on some of the major challenges in university education … They have drawn together a strong team of active academics who are producing teaching materials that are novel in the breadth of their approach.'

Prof Lord Broers,
former Vice-Chancellor of the University of Cambridge

'The Macat vision is exceptionally exciting. It focuses upon new modes of learning which analyse and explain seminal texts which have profoundly influenced world thinking and so social and economic development. It promotes the kind of critical thinking which is essential for any society and economy. This is the learning of the future.'

Rt Hon Charles Clarke, former UK Secretary of State for Education

'The Macat analyses provide immediate access to the critical conversation surrounding the books that have shaped their respective discipline, which will make them an invaluable resource to all of those, students and teachers, working in the field.'

Professor William Tronzo, University of California at San Diego

WAYS IN TO THE TEXT

KEY POINTS

- Benedict Anderson is an influential and well-respected modernist* scholar of nationalism studies*—a subfield of the social sciences that draws on the aims and methods of different academic disciplines; in the field of nationalism studies, modernists reject the view that nations are "natural" and ancient.

- Anderson's *Imagined Communities* argues that our contemporary idea of nations and nationalism*—devotion to the interests of a particular nation-state—has its origin in the decline of religion and the advent of the printing press,* which created new ways for people to think, interact, and imagine their connections and boundaries.

- When it was published in 1983, *Imagined Communities* was considered groundbreaking; its original stance has made it one of the key texts in nationalism studies.

Who Is Benedict Anderson?

Irish scholar Benedict Anderson, the author of *Imagined Communities* (1983), was born in 1936 in Kunming, China to an English mother and an Irish father. His family life and formative experiences had a profound impact on the thinker he would later become. At the age of five, he and his family moved to the United States, then to Ireland, and later to the United Kingdom. Anderson was educated at Eton College,* an elite boarding school in England. He went on to study at Cambridge University, where he earned a Bachelor of Arts degree in classics in 1957, and received his PhD in government from Cornell University, in the United States in 1967. At Cornell, he studied under the guidance of George Kahin,* a renowned American scholar of Southeast Asia and an activist who opposed America's involvement in the Vietnam War.* Anderson's postgraduate research consisted of fieldwork in Indonesia and resulted in two important publications: *A Preliminary Analysis of the October 1, 1965, Coup in Indonesia* (also known as the "Cornell Paper") (1971), and *Java in a Time of Revolution: Occupation and Resistance 1944–1946* (1972), an analysis of the 1945 youth revolution in Indonesia against Japanese occupation.

Southeast Asia remains the central focus of Anderson's teaching and an area of avid personal interest for him. He is currently Aaron L. Binencorb Professor Emeritus of International Studies at Cornell University, where he has taught since 1965, and he has served as director of the university's prestigious modern Indonesia program.

While Anderson is an established academic with many important works to his name, *Imagined Communities* was his breakthrough work that attracted a popular international readership.

His brother, Perry Anderson,* is also a renowned academic, working as a professor of history and sociology at the University of California, Los Angeles, and has served as the editor of the *New Left Review*.*

What Does *Imagined Communities* Say?

Imagined Communities argues that the invention in the fifteenth century of the printing press—a moveable type machine that allowed for the cheap mass production of books—radically transformed society in ways that helped create the modern nation and nationalism. Prior to this, books were produced by hand and usually written in Latin, making them too expensive and linguistically inaccessible to ordinary people. However, the mass production of books made them suddenly affordable, and local vernaculars—or languages—gradually overtook Latin in print. This allowed speakers of diverse local dialects to communicate and understand each other, which resulted in new ways of thinking. Later, the printing press allowed the ideas of Enlightenment* thinkers to reach audiences beyond the noble elites and the clergy.

The Enlightenment was a philosophical movement that developed in Europe in the late seventeenth and eighteenth century. It emphasized the use of reason to scrutinize previously accepted orthodoxies* and traditions, and brought about many important humanitarian reforms. It stressed progress, liberty, and equality. In the Americas, where colonial settlers were subject to injustices from the European powers who ruled them, including high taxes and inadequate political representation, these ideas helped fuel a growing desire for self-sufficiency and self-rule.

Anderson also sees a change in the popular notion of time as a result of both the decline of religion that came with Enlightenment thought, and the new availability of reading material after the advent of the printing press. With the authority of time as presented in the Bible now subject to skepticism (or seen, at least, as less literal than before), a more standardized concept of time based on the clock, calendar, books, and newspapers filled this void of continuity. This allowed individuals to identify with others outside their immediate surroundings and to create "imagined communities" with territorial limits set by shared language and official state time. Anderson explains that these new identifications formed an "imagined, inherently limited and sovereign* political community" in which "members of even the smallest nation will never know most of their fellow members, meet, or even hear of them, yet in the minds of each lives the image of their communion."[1]

In Anderson's interpretation, common people could now feel pride or shame in the actions of others in a much wider sphere beyond the people they know, and outwards into the "imagined community" or nation. Shared, secular time and an accessible, common literature helped foster a sense of loyalty so great that, where people were once willing to die in the name of religion (as in the medieval European military incursions in the Middle East known as the Crusades), they were now willing to give up their lives for their nation.

Imagined Communities made several important and unique contributions to the field of nationalism studies. Before Anderson, no scholar had linked capitalism* (an economic system based on private ownership, private enterprise, and the maximization of profit), print language, and nationalism in such a coherent way. This account of the link between technology, ideology, and social change also considers individuals' profound emotional bond to their nation and their willingness to sacrifice themselves in its name. While this has been addressed by other scholars, such as the nationalism scholar Anthony Smith,* the way that Anderson describes nationalism as a social construction for political and economic ends is original.

The scope and perspective of this work have had a lasting effect on its field. It focuses on nationalist movements in parts of the world that had previously been ignored, representing a significant and timely break in the Eurocentrism* of nationalism studies (that is, the tendency of nationalism studies to address predominantly European issues). Similarly, while most scholars argue that nationhood started in Europe, Anderson turns this assumption on its head and asserts that it originated among European descendants in the Americas.

According to Anderson, settler "nationalists" used language to build communities to challenge what they saw as imperialist oppression. This triggered the European powers to develop an *official* nationalism, which was a reactionary counter-narrative aimed at safeguarding their domination. These ideas paved the way for further research on the relationship between European colonizers and "Third World"* nationalism. Finally, Anderson's book described the nation as an "inherently limited and sovereign imagined community" and, unlike the work of other modernists, distinguished nations by the ways in which they are imagined.

Why Does *Imagined Communities* Matter?

Imagined Communities represents one of the cornerstones of modernist thought in nationalism studies. Modernists reject the view put forth by primordialists* that nations are "natural" and date back to the beginning of time. They also reject the perspective of ethno-symbolists that modern nations and nationalism stem from the pre-modern era (roughly, the period before 1500). In contrast, modernists view the nation as a political and social creation that evolved alongside capitalism from the sixteenth century onwards.

Anderson links the development of capitalism and print language with the decline of religion, European dynasties,* and imperialist culture—the culture of empire building through colonial conquest—to explain how nations and nationalism have evolved in the modern era. He does this in order to address what he perceives as a shortcoming of Marxist* theory.

Karl Marx,* the founder of Marxist thought, was an internationalist who called on workers everywhere, regardless of nationality, to unite on the basis of class interests to overthrow capitalism, their common enemy. Anderson finds this problematic; since 1945, he points out, Asian socialist* revolutions—popular uprisings that draw on Marxist economic theory—have been based on a discourse of nationalism and national heroes rather than class struggle (the latter term referring, very roughly, to the conflict of interest between working people and the wealthy, who govern).

For three decades, *Imagined Communities* has provided a springboard for research and debate within academia and beyond. It has sold over a quarter of a million copies and has been published in 29 languages in 33 countries.[2] Today it remains one of the most frequently cited texts in the humanities and social sciences.[3] It continues to play a leading role in the evolving understanding of nationhood, and remains an essential read for students in many disciplines.

In the academic world, the text normally either serves as literature on which to build a similar argument that nations and nationalism are a social construction of the modern era, or it provides a starting point for those who wish to refute aspects of Anderson's argument. Anthony Smith is one example of a scholar who takes issue with Anderson and claims that nation and nationalism stem from pre-modern conditions.

Furthermore, because of Anderson's interdisciplinary focus (that is, the way in which he draws on the aims and methods of different academic fields in the course of his research and analysis), *Imagined Communities* has proved indispensable to thinkers in a range of disciplines from anthropology to postcolonial* studies.

NOTES

1 Benedict Anderson, *Imagined Communities* (London and New York: Verso, 2006), 6.

2 Anderson, *Imagined Communities*, 207.

3 Thomson Reuters, *ISI Web of Science* (New York: Thomson Reuters, 2007).

SECTION 1
INFLUENCES

MODULE 1
THE AUTHOR AND THE
HISTORICAL CONTEXT

KEY POINTS

- *Imagined Communities* is one of the most cited texts in the humanities and social sciences. Since its publication, it has provided a basis for the advancement of scholarship and debate on nations and nationalism* (dedication to the interests of a specific nation, frequently expressed through political organization).

- Anderson's Irish heritage and citizenship influenced his understanding and representation of nations and nationalism.

- Key global events, including the Suez Crisis* (1956), in the course of which Britain and France attempted to regain Western control of the Suez canal in Egypt, and the Vietnam War* (1954–75), in which the United States fought against the communist forces of North Vietnam, partly shaped the author's interest in nations and nationalism and his representation of them in *Imagined Communities.*

Why Read This Text?

Since its publication in 1983, Benedict Anderson's *Imagined Communities* has provoked important debate among scholars in the field of politics and opened new ways of thinking about the origins and operation of nationalism both inside the academic sphere and in the wider public. The text fits the modernist* and constructivist* schools of nationalism studies, since both agree that nations and nationalism are political and social creations of the modern era.

❝ Like many others I was active in the anti-Vietnam War* movement, and more and more regarded myself as a sort of anarchistic* leftist. It was also in this period that I started to read the main Marxist* classics of the nineteenth century and twentieth century, especially Marx* and Lenin,* partly because I enjoyed their writing style. At that point my plan was to spend the rest of my life as a scholar and teacher about Indonesia, and [Southeast] Asia. ❞

Benedict Anderson, in "Interview with Benedict Anderson, 'We Study Empires as We Do Dinosaurs': Nations, Nationalism, and Empire in a Critical Perspective"

Anderson links this to the development of industrial capitalism* (the economic model on which the West as we know it today was founded) and to the socialization that emerged from the spread of printed publications in everyday language.

In the text, Anderson analyzes several important themes, but with an original focus. The themes include the decline of religion; the link between capitalism, print language, and nationalism; the emotional bond between individuals and their nations; the interplay between European imperialism* (empire-building) and Third World* nationalism (the nationalism of developing nations); the origins and development of nations and nationalism in the Americas; and the ways in which nations can be distinguished by how they are collectively imagined.

Imagined Communities has sold over a quarter of a million copies and has been published in 29 languages in 33 countries.[2] It is currently one of the most frequently cited texts in the humanities and social sciences, and it is an important reference point in ongoing scholarship and debate. Consequently, it remains an essential read for students in different academic disciplines, particularly nationalism studies,* and for general readers looking for different ways of understanding nations and nationalism in the modern era.

Author's Life

Benedict Anderson's heritage and citizenship, as well as the variety of places and contexts in which he grew up and studied, have had a noticeable effect on his later ideas and approach to his subject matter. His father's side of the family, the O'Gormans, was of mixed Irish and Anglo-Irish origins, and active in Irish nationalist politics. One of his relatives was imprisoned for taking part in the United Irishmen's Rebellion of 1798* (an uprising that sought universal male suffrage and the elimination of British rule in Ireland). Another was the secretary of the Irish political leader Daniel O'Connell's* Catholic* Association, and fought for social and political equality for Roman Catholics under British colonial rule. Because of these Irish nationalist roots, although he was educated in England from the age of 11, he never considered himself English.[3]

A consciousness of politics and social justice remained strong into his adulthood. Anderson recalls a day in Cambridge in 1956, when he was an undergraduate, when a group of upper-class English students, chanting "God Save the Queen," assaulted a group of Sri Lankans demonstrating against Britain's invasion of Egypt in its attempt to gain control of the Suez canal, a strategically important link between the Mediterranean and the Red Sea, recently incorporated into the Egyptian state by the nation's president. "The scene seemed incomprehensible and I feebly tried to get the educated louts to stop," Anderson recalled. "My spectacles were smacked off my face, and so, by chance, I joined the column of the assaulted."[4] Motivated by his family's involvement in Irish nationalist resistance, the global tumult sparked by the process of decolonization,* and his experience at Cornell University in the United States being tutored by experts on Southeast Asia, Anderson shifted his focus as a postgraduate from classics to nationalism studies.

In 1967, Anderson began his PhD at Cornell University, enrolling in the recently created Modern Indonesian Studies program. His academic work subsequently focused on key events in Indonesia, and the Asian region more broadly, including the 1965 military coup in Indonesia; the Vietnam War (1954–75); and the armed conflicts in Southeast Asia between 1978 and 1979. Observing these serious regional conflicts as a scholar, Anderson was led to wonder why these supposedly socialist* struggles were being waged around a discourse of nationalism and national heroes rather than a discourse of class struggle, as one might have expected given that Marxist theory generally underpins much socialist argument and policy. As a doctoral student, he studied under the supervision of George Kahin,* a leading American academic on Southeast Asia and an activist who protested against America's involvement in Vietnam.

Author's Background

It is no coincidence that a number of eminent works on nationalism appeared during the late 1970s and early 1980s, a period that saw the resurgence of ethno-nationalism* (the desire of an ethnic community to have complete control over its political, economic, and social affairs) and ethnic conflict, and the renewed prominence of ideological politics. The Vietnam War, political disorder in Cambodia, negotiations for devolution* (the process of transferring power from the central government to sub-national governments) in the United Kingdom, Catalonian and Basque nationalism in Spain, Québécois nationalism in Canada, and ethno-political disputes following decolonization in Africa and Asia were all striking contemporary developments.

The 1978–9 Iranian Revolution,* which saw the overthrow of a Western-backed monarch, Shah* Mohammad Reza Pahlavi,* and his replacement with an Islamic Republic,* was another critical moment in late twentieth-century nationalism with particularly far-reaching consequences. It showed the power of religion as a uniting force in challenging Western imperialism and transforming society. In the United States and the United Kingdom, Ronald Reagan* and Margaret Thatcher* took office as president and prime minister respectively, bringing with them a new political and economic vision of the world based on free-market* values—that is, the social and economic values of unfettered capitalism—following the economic crisis of the 1970s.

From the 1950s onwards, as many nations claimed their independence from the European nations that had colonized them, and new states in Africa and Asia were formed, modernist scholarship on nations and nationalism emerged in different scholarly fields. Now the view of nations as a modern phenomenon posed a serious challenge to the primordialist* belief, held by many politicians and historians, that nations have existed since time immemorial. The scholars Elie Kedourie,* Tom Nairn,* Ernest Gellner,* Eric Hobsbawm,* and others built on previous research by thinkers such as Hans Kohn,* Carlton Hayes,* Hugh Seton-Watson,* and Karl Deutsch,* to offer new insight into the origins and development of nations and nationalism.

NOTES

1   Thomson Reuters, *ISI Web of Science* (New York: Thomson Reuters, 2007).

2   Benedict Anderson, *Imagined Communities* (London and New York: Verso, 2006), 207.

3   Benedict Anderson, *Language and Power: Exploring Political Cultures in Indonesia* (Ithaca, NY: Cornell University Press, 1990), 14

4   Anderson, *Language and Power*, 207.

MODULE 2
ACADEMIC CONTEXT

KEY POINTS

- Benedict Anderson is a historical materialist,* meaning that he studies political, social, and cultural transformations in relation to economics and class struggle.

- Published in the context of a surge in ethnic conflicts and ideological politics, *Imagined Communities* contributed to a body of scholarship aimed at mapping the origins of nations and nationalism.*

- *Imagined Communities* argues that nations and nationalism are political and social creations of the modern era that have developed alongside capitalism.* This challenges the belief that nations and nationalism are natural or stem from the pre-modern era.

The Work in its Context

Benedict Anderson is a historical materialist, a thinker who focuses on the relationship between social change and the economic, material conditions within a given society, as well as on the relationship between social classes. His regular references to the power of print capitalism*—a concept he uses to describe the conditions under which imagined communities ("nations") became possible—reflects his understanding of the role played by technology and the press in dividing industrial societies into two basic groups: those who control the means of production* (the resources and tools required to manufacture goods) and those who sell their labor power and produce goods (workers). In this sense, he attributes important transformations in social institutions and in the evolution of ideas to economics and class struggle.

> ❝ I was influenced (not always positively) by Tom
> Nairn's* 'Scottish nationalist book' *The Breakup of
> Britain* and wanted to join the battle—on his side—in
> the intellectual controversy the book aroused. ❞
>
> Benedict Anderson, in Semyonov Alexander, "Interview with Benedict
> Anderson, 'We Study Empires as We Do Dinosaurs': Nations, Nationalism,
> and Empire in a Critical Perspective"

At the same time, he describes nationalism in cultural terms. *Imagined Communities* was an attempt, within the broader context of the Cold War*—the period of "tension" and ideological conflict between the United States and Soviet Union* that so marked the world between 1946 and 1991—to link theories of nationalism with Marxist* thought (the social and economic analyses offered by the economist and political philosopher Karl Marx).* He did this in order to challenge Euro-American imperialism* (the cultural and economic empire-building of the United States and Europe) and represent voices that he felt had been neglected by Eurocentric* scholarship (scholarship that focused almost exclusively on issues that concerned Europe).

In *Imagined Communities*, Anderson aimed to build on the Scottish nationalist theorist Tom Nairn's seminal work *The Break-up of Britain: Crisis and Neo-Nationalism* (1977) by attempting to close a long-standing gap between Marxist theory and nationalism, an issue he felt Marxists had historically "elided, rather than confronted."[1] In the *Communist Manifesto* (1848), Karl Marx and Friedrich Engels* argued that the working classes have no country and must unite across national borders against the common enemy: capitalism—the economic system in which resources and industry are held in private hands. This, in Anderson's view, overlooked the power of nationalism as a uniting force.

Overview of the Field

As with the nationalism scholar John Breuilly's* *Nationalism and the State* (1982), the British Czech social philosopher Ernest Gellner's* *Nations and Nationalism* (1983), and *The Invention of Tradition* (1983), edited by historians Eric Hobsbawm* and Terrence Ranger,* Anderson's *Imagined Communities* is modernist* in that it challenges those who argue that nations stem from the pre-modern period. However, Anderson differentiates himself from his modernist colleagues by linking nations and nationalism to the evolution of print language and anti-colonial resistance in the Americas. *Imagined Communities* is also a constructivist* text in that Anderson portrays the formation of nations as an evolving process of identity formation, socially constructed through two interlinked factors: human agency (or influence) and structural conditions. For constructivists, these two concepts can only exist together. Take language, for example. Established structures such as grammar and syntax exist; however, people ultimately sustain or modify these. One may sustain, for example, the sentence "My son and I are teachers," or one might modify this incorrectly in slang as follows: "Me and my son are teachers." While conversations involve certain rules such as syntax that are necessary for us to understand each other, language can still be manipulated by the speakers; while structures influence behavior, they are sustainable and modifiable through human actions.

Anderson also uses comparative methodology in that he analyzes different geographical contexts, and looks at the ways in which nations, while they often model themselves on others, imagine themselves in different ways. Finally, he provides some degree of institutional analysis* through his portrayal of the census (population surveys), maps, and museums as tools used by European colonial powers to build the narrative of nation they needed to counter the nationalism growing in colonial communities outside the mother country.

Academic Influences

Anderson's outlook was influenced by a number of distinguished intellectuals. As he once recalled, "three good Germans, Karl Marx, Walter Benjamin* and Erich Auerbach,* helped me think about the modern world."[2] Walter Benjamin was a deeply influential cultural critic and philosopher; Erich Auerbach was a distinguished scholar of literature. During a critical stage of intellectual development at Cornell University, Anderson benefited from the ideas and encouragement of the Southeast Asia scholar George Kahin,* the linguistics professor John Echols,* and the scholar of Indonesian culture, Claire Holt.*

His decision to publish *Imagined Communities* with Verso (formerly New Left Books, and noted for publishing books emphasizing left-wing political analysis) was influenced by his brother Perry Anderson,* a well-known academic and powerful figure at the *New Left Review,* and by its former editor, Anthony Barnett.*

Anderson was also influenced by the large amount of modernist scholarship on nations and nationalism that emerged in Britain, and to a lesser extent in the United States, in the late 1970s and early 1980s. This included important works by Gellner, Hobsbawm, Ranger, and Breuilly. All of these works challenged claims that nations and nationalism were of pre-modern origin.

While all of these scholars belong to the modernist school of thought, there are important differences between them. Gellner studied nationalism from a sociological perspective and argued that nations developed after the transition from an agricultural economy to an industrial one; Hobsbawm showed how some customs and traditions that are widely regarded as ancient are in reality modern and socially constructed; and Breuilly emphasized the importance of political institutions and geopolitics* (the study of how political and economic geography determine politics and international relations) in shaping the development of nations and nationalism.

Anderson differentiated himself from Gellner and Hobsbawm by arguing that imagined communities should be judged not in terms of real versus false (Gellner's "fabrication" and Hobsbawm's "invented traditions"), but rather by the different ways in which communities are conceived in a shared imagination through a common print language. In addition, while Gellner and Hobsbawm are generally hostile towards nationalism, highlighting its tendency to provoke conflict, Anderson is more interested in its positive power to unite populations.

NOTES

1   Benedict Anderson, *Imagined Communities* (London and New York: Verso, 2006), 3.

2   Benedict Anderson, *Language and Power: Exploring Political Cultures in Indonesia* (Ithaca, NY: Cornell University Press, 1990), 14.

MODULE 3
THE PROBLEM

KEY POINTS

- In the late 1970s and early 1980s, a number of scholars attempted to gain a deeper understanding of the origins and development of nations and nationalism due to a resurgence of ethnic and ideological conflicts around the world.

- At the time, there were two main schools of thought on the origins and development of nations and nationalism, comprised of those who believed they were wholly modern creations, and those who believed that they stemmed from the pre-modern era.

- Anderson contributed to this evolving debate by explaining the links between the economic and social system of capitalism,* print language, and the development of nations and nationalism.

Core Question

The core research question Benedict Anderson poses in *Imagined Communities* is: why have all successful revolutions since World War II* been framed in national terms rather than through a historical materialist* (or Marxist)* perspective centered on class struggle? In other words, why have nationalist ideas been more obviously important to these revolutions than ideas taken from the analysis of social and economic history outlined by Karl Marx?* In his analysis, Anderson points to several geographical examples, with a particular focus on Southeast Asian contexts.

In his discussion of the power of nationalism, Anderson also addresses a number of key sub-questions. Among these are: Where did

> ❝ Nation, nationality, nationalism*—all have proved notoriously difficult to define, let alone analyze. In contrast to the immense influence that nationalism has exerted on the modern world, plausible theory about it is conspicuously meager. ❞
>
> Benedict Anderson, *Imagined Communities*

nations and nationalism originate? Why and how did they evolve? Are they ancient or modern phenomena? What creates the profound emotional bond between individuals and their nations? How is nationalism reproduced? And what distinguishes one nation from another?

Anderson asked these key questions against the backdrop of a resurgence of nationalism and ethnic conflict in different parts of the world and an accentuation of ideological politics in the United States and the United Kingdom, where the right-wing political leaders Ronald Reagan* and Margaret Thatcher* were reshaping their nations' political, economic, and social systems. In addressing these questions, the author concludes that nations and nationalism are wholly modern creations that stem from important political, economic, social, and cultural transformations from the fifteenth century onwards. This position contributed to the growing body of modernist* scholarship that challenged the idea that nations had existed since the beginning of time, or at least since the pre-modern era.

The Participants

Building on the works of Hans Kohn,* Carlton Hayes,* Elie Kedourie,* Tom Nairn,* Eric Hobsbawm,* and other scholars, Anderson addresses a perceived research gap between Marxism and nationalism. He does this through an original means—by focusing both on print capitalism* (his idea that nations emerged along with the printing of books in common vernacular languages and the simultaneous development of market capitalism) and on "creole"* revolutionary movements against European imperial powers in the Americas; two factors that until that point had been largely overlooked in academic research. In doing so, he highlights the prominence of culture and imagination in building nationalism and national heroes, over a focus on class as the basis of revolutionary struggles.

In the text, the term "creoles" refers to settler populations in the Americas with European roots who, influenced by Enlightenment* ideas now accessible in affordable books printed in everyday language, developed a sense of nationhood in response to their unfair treatment by European imperialism.* This then triggered the deliberate reactionary construction of official nationalism by European dynastic rulers in an attempt to safeguard their power and privilege over the colonies. This construction of nationalism, whereby it originated in creole settler populations, upended the earlier assumption that nationalism was a product of European dynastic powers.

Anderson is positioned as a major contributor to the modernist school of thought, as well as to the schools of constructivism* (according to which nations and nationalism are social constructions of the modern era) and historical materialism* (according to which social and economic factors such as class struggle were the driving force behind historical events). This is due to his original focus on: the link between capitalism, print language, and nationalism; the emotional bond between individuals and their nation; the interplay between European imperialism and "Third World"* nationalism; the historical relevance of the Americas in fostering nations and nationalism; and the distinction between nations in terms of the ways in which they are imagined.

The Contemporary Debate

Imagined Communities emerged from an important debate at the time within the New Left*—a social and political movement that emerged in the 1960s and 1970s seeking progressive social reforms—about the causes and significance of contemporary global events.

In 1977, the Scottish scholar of nationalism Tom Nairn, then a Marxist, published his book *The Break-up of Britain*, which focused on the resurgence of Scottish nationalism and a desire among many Scots for independence. In it, he argued: "The theory of nationalism is Marxism's greatest historical failure. It may have others as well, and some of these have been more debated … yet none of these is as important, as fundamental, as the problem of nationalism, either in theory or in political practice."[1] In 1981, in the postscript of his revised edition, Nairn stated: "On one side a bourgeois nationalism* denied region and class altogether; on the other a lumpen socialism* denied nationality any progressive significance whatever (unless it ran through the middle of the English Channel)."[2] "Lumpen socialism" here describes a dogmatic political belief according to which there can be very little that is positive about nationalism at all.

In the influential journal *New Left Review*,* the Marxist historian Eric Hobsbawm responded to this in the article "Some Reflections on 'The Break-up of Britain'," in which he offered a sharp attack on Nairn's critique of Marxist thought and his support for Scottish independence:

"Nationalism has been a great puzzle to (non-nationalist) politicians and theorists ever since its invention, not only because it is both powerful and devoid of any discernible rational theory, but also because its shape and function are constantly changing … The real danger for Marxists [like Nairn] is the temptation to welcome nationalism as an ideology and program rather than realistically to accept it as a fact." In concluding, and in specific reference to Nairn, Hobsbawm echoed the words of the Russian revolutionary leader Vladimir Lenin:* "do not paint nationalism red."[3]

This ideological disagreement between two of the most prominent writers of the New Left was partly responsible for provoking *Imagined Communities*. In it, Anderson sought to critically support Nairn's central argument that classical Marxism* had failed to consider the historical–political potential of nationalism as a unifying force. He does this by drawing links between the ways nationalism emerged, how it evolved through the modern era, how it was adapted across space and time in relation to capitalism and print language, and why it fostered such strong emotional bonds between individuals who perceived themselves as part of "imagined communities."

The decision to write *Imagined Communities* was also provoked by the political conflicts in Indochina (Southeast Asia) in 1978–9, which led the author to ask why brutal wars were taking place between so-called socialist regimes when Marxist philosophy calls them to unite across national borders, and why the fighters in these battles justified their bloodshed through discourses of nationalism rather than as Marxist class struggle.

NOTES

1   Tom Nairn, *The Break-up of Britain* (London: New Left Books, 1977), 329.

2   Tom Nairn, *The Break-up of Britain*, second edition (London: Verso, 1981), 397–8.

3   Eric Hobsbawm, "Some Reflections on 'The Break-up of Britain,'" *New Left Review* 105, no. 5 (1977): 3.

MODULE 4
THE AUTHOR'S CONTRIBUTION

KEY POINTS

- Anderson's core idea in *Imagined Communities* is that nations and nationalism* are wholly modern creations that emerged from the development of print capitalism—that is, the introduction of printing in common languages, which united different local dialects to create national languages and a national "conversation."

- This view made an important contribution to modernist* thought in nationalism studies,* and has since served as a foundation for further scholarship and debate.

- Anderson's argument drew from existing scholarship and debates on nations and nationalism and offered a novel, modernist perspective on the subject.

Author's Aims

Imagined Communities reflects Benedict Anderson's interdisciplinary background as an anthropologist, historian, literary scholar, and political scientist. It also highlights his emotional attachment to both Ireland and Southeast Asia. The text was written for a general, well-educated public, and seeks to make a substantial contribution to contemporary leftist thinking, especially within the United Kingdom and Ireland.

Anderson's literary interests, experiences gained in the different parts of the world in which he lived, and close contact with well-known anthropologists all contributed to his approach, whereby he placed a greater emphasis on culture and language than his contemporaries and predecessors such as the British Czech social

> ❝ Print-capitalism* gave a new fixity to language, which in the long run helped to build that image of antiquity so central to the subjective idea of the nation. ❞
>
> Benedict Anderson, *Imagined Communities*

philosopher Ernest Gellner,* the Marxist* historian Eric Hobsbawm,* and the nationalism scholar Anthony Smith.* It was also important to Anderson that the socioeconomic components were fully analyzed through his use of a Marxist,* historical materialist* approach to his subject matter—that is, an approach founded on the assumption that history is driven by social and economic factors such as class struggle.

Anderson aimed to contribute to the debate conducted in the late 1970s between the Scottish nationalism theorist Tom Nairn* and Eric Hobsbawm in a journal called the *New Left Review** regarding the relationship between the social system derived from Marxism and nationalism. He also sought to show that Gellner's link between industrialization* and nationalism in his work *Thought and Change* (1964) was too simplistic. As Anderson puts it: "The thesis was difficult to accept given the early appearance of nationalism in the Americas at a time when industrialism did not exist there. It was also difficult to accept because it did not explain why nationalism mattered so emotionally to people … He wholly underestimated the power of writing, and the way that writing moved much faster than industrialism."[1]

Since its publication, *Imagined Communities* has sold over a quarter of a million copies,[2] and has been published in 33 countries,[3] far surpassing the author's expectations. In fact, Anderson points out in the afterword of his second edition (1991) and last revised edition (2006) that he never expected that it would become a university-level textbook and a global point of reference in the social sciences.

Approach

In *Imagined Communities*, Benedict Anderson sought to better understand the unclear relationship between Marxist thought and nationalism. Seeking to challenge American and British imperialism,* he offers a modernist, deliberately non-Eurocentric* approach to the origins and evolution of nationhood and nationalism that emphasizes the agency, or power to act, of colonial subjects.

His two main focal points are: the development from the early sixteenth century onwards of print capitalism—a term he uses to describe the spreading of progressive ideas through printed texts; and anti-colonial revolutions in the Americas against European imperial powers such as the British, Spanish, and French empires. In addressing these themes, his intent is not to offer an in-depth critique of Marxism or to create an all-encompassing theory of nationalism based on an exhaustive survey of previous literature. Instead, he offers a composite picture of original and overlapping points of reflection on the sources and origins of nationhood and nationalism, their changing meanings across space and time, their political and social construction, and the power of emotion and imagination in bonding communities.

Anderson's novel approach to the origins of nationalism centers on its link to the rise of print capitalism. From the early sixteenth century, the availability of books in common languages helped spread ideas formulated by thinkers of the European intellectual current known as the Enlightenment,* bringing the notions of personal liberty, rationalism,* and secularism* to ordinary people, and in this way providing the basic principles on which colonial independence movements were founded. The decline of religion made possible new conceptions of time that were no longer rooted in the biblical stories of the origins of man at one end, and eternal salvation or damnation on the other. Out of this vacuum, people began to imagine the past, present, and future of the nation as the dominant shared narrative of continuity. While Anderson sees these basic structures as common among modern notions of nationhood, the specific ways in which these things are socially constructed and imagined are what distinguish one nation from another.

Contribution in Context

Anderson addresses what he perceives as a failure of Marxist analysis to address either the role of print capitalism in the history of nationalism or the anti-colonial revolutionary movements against European imperial powers in the Americas—two factors that, until this point, had been largely underexplored in scholarly inquiry.

For Anderson, print capitalism describes the conditions under which imagined communities (that is, nations) became possible. This occurred, he argues, only after the introduction of printing in languages other than Latin in the early sixteenth century, following the invention of the printing press* in the fifteenth century; this in turn united different local dialects and created common languages and discourses.

Anderson was successful in reaching his intended audience and in presenting an interdisciplinary study that advanced modernist thinking about nations and nationalism. The book's commercial success has surpassed that of the renowned Ernest Gellner's *Nations and Nationalism*, also published in 1983, which has to date sold an estimated 160,000 copies.[4] In addition, Anderson is the only nationalism scholar included in the list *ISI Web of Science* (2007), published by Thomson Reuters, of the most cited authors of books in the humanities. These two facts show the enduring relevance of *Imagined Communities* as a seminal text in the humanities and social sciences.

NOTES

1   Benedict Anderson, in Semyonov Alexander, "Interview with Benedict Anderson, 'We Study Empires as We Do Dinosaurs': Nations, Nationalism, and Empire in a Critical Perspective," *Ab Imperio* 3 (2003): 57–73.

2   For more detail, see, Verso Books, accessed June 5, 2013, www.versobooks.com/books/60–imagined-communities.

3   Benedict Anderson, *Imagined Communities* (London and New York: Verso, 2006), 207.

4   Ernest Gellner, *Nations and Nationalism* (Ithaca, NY: Cornell University Press, 1983).

SECTION 2
IDEAS

MODULE 5
MAIN IDEAS

KEY POINTS

- Anderson's main argument is that the diffusion of progressive ideas through printed texts in commonly spoken languages was key to the development of nations—"imagined communities"—in the Americas.

- He presents his themes through a mosaic of points of reflection on the origins and development of nations and nationalism* in the Americas, Europe, and elsewhere.

- While many theorists tend to view nationalism only as a force that excludes certain populations and encourages insularity, Anderson recognizes its potential as a positive, uniting force.

Key Themes

Benedict Anderson's *Imagined Communities* focuses on the spread of the rational and progressive ideas of the period of European intellectual history known as the Enlightenment* through affordable books in common languages, the rise of capitalism,* and changes in understandings of the nature of time thanks to the growth of secular (that is, non-religious) thought.

For Anderson, these concurrent developments led to the creation and evolution of nations and nationalism in the Americas, Europe, and Southeast Asia, and helped unite these "imagined communities" in their struggles against imperialist* rule.

Anderson describes how, from the 1500s onwards, after the invention of the printing press,* printing in the vernacular—that is, in common languages—took over from use of Latin and other sacred script languages. This allowed greater communication among ordinary

> ❝ I propose the following definition of the nation: it is an imagined political community—and imagined as both inherently limited and sovereign* ... It is *imagined* because the members of even the smallest nation will never know most of their fellow members, meet them, or even hear of them, yet in the mind of each lives the image of their communion. ❞
>
> Benedict Anderson, *Imagined Communities*

people and promoted new ways of thinking. Furthermore, he shows how the spread of Enlightenment ideas of progress, liberty, and equality through printed language spurred European descendants in the Americas to challenge European imperial domination. In particular, he highlights the important role local merchants, officials, and operators of print machinery played in this process. He argues that this revolutionary spirit responded to colonial oppression and led to a desire among many in the colonies for self-rule.

Anderson also describes the parallel decline of religion during this period. He shows how this led people to question the certainty of eternal salvation and with it, its position marking the end of time, and he challenged the long-standing religious link connecting past generations with current and future ones. Printed material brought in a secular concept of time based on the clock, calendar, books, and newspapers, which filled this void. Now individuals could identify with others both within and beyond their immediate environment, united by literature in a common language and a shared sense of time within somewhat arbitrary territorial limits. This created a new sense of connection, along with feelings of happiness, pride, shame, and anger over the actions of others and, with it, the idea that one should be willing to die for one's "nation."

Exploring the Ideas

Anderson's principal theoretical aim is to address the gap between Marxism* and nationalism by accounting for the sources and origins of the latter, its evolution, its adaptation across time and space, and its power as a uniting force among individuals. He does this through his analysis of print capitalism* and anti-colonial (creole)* revolutionary movements against European imperial powers in the Americas.

In addressing this gap between Marxism and nationalism, *Imagined Communities* uses conflict among Asian socialist* regimes, particularly during the period of 1978–9 in Indochina—southeast Asia—to consider these ideas in a new context. Here, the key question Anderson contemplates is: why has every successful revolution since World War II* defined itself in national terms rather than as class struggle, as Marxist theory would predict?

In the initial stages of the text, in contrast to primordialists* (who argue that nations are natural and ancient), perennialists* (who argue that nations are ancient but are not natural—that is, they are not based on sociobiological origins), and ethno-symbolists* (who argue that modern nations and nationalism stem from pre-modern conditions), Anderson presents a modernist interpretation of nationhood and nationalism as phenomena linked to the spread of print capitalism.

He takes this further by explaining that the emotional attachment to religious identity was eventually replaced by an emotional attachment to nation that was so strong that people were willing to sacrifice their lives for it. Here, he argues that the sense of immortality that is largely ignored by liberalism* (a very broad current of ideas that emphasize individual liberty) and Marxism, and that was once offered by religion and dynastic succession (the procession of kings and queens), is now imagined within the concept of nationhood.

Anderson asserts that nationalism evolved as a spontaneous, complex crossing of historical experiences and subsequently became "modular"*—that is, capable of being reproduced in different forms by other nations as print capitalism gave people ready access to news of events in other locations (indeed, in other nations).

Imagined Communities attributes the rise of nationalism to: the development of print language and print capitalism, which propelled Enlightenment ideas into the popular imagination; the uniting of populations through shared common language; and a secular sense of time that brought about an emotional bond between individuals and the nation—the "imagined community"—they collectively made.

Colonialism* (the settling of one nation by another and the social and political consequences that arise from it) abruptly widened the cultural and geographical horizons and brought diverse communities into contact for the first time. At the same time, Enlightenment secularism* prompted many to question the absolute authority of religious notions of time and to seek a sense of continuity through a bond with their nation instead.

For Anderson, nationhood was first developed in the Americas by anti-colonialists (creoles), who, inspired by Enlightenment philosophy, were reacting against the heavy taxation and other forms of oppression at the hands of European colonial powers. This triggered an official response from European leaders, who sought to safeguard their aristocratic* power and privileges over their territories—in other words, the nobility acted to preserve their own interests.

Anderson then turns to nationalism in colonial Asia and Africa during the period of European decolonization,* during which nations claimed their independence, following World War II.* He argues that European and American national histories taught in colonial classrooms, and reinforced through institutions such as museums, further inspired these colonies to seek independence from European powers. In this way, nationalist models from the Americas and Europe were "copied, adapted, and improved upon" by colonial subjects elsewhere, who took advantage of new and more advanced forms of communication, such as the radio and mass-produced images, to complement or bypass print in fostering their own imagined communities.[1]

Language and Expression

The book's title conveys Anderson's original concept—that nations are socially constructed communities that stem from print capitalism and are formed around common languages and discourses (that is, roughly, "national conversations.") They are *imagined* by people who perceive themselves as part of these communities, and are in contrast to "real" communities based on daily, face-to-face interaction.

Relevant to readers from disciplines as diverse as history and political science, Anderson's argument is clear, concise, and novel; while certain terms may seem complex to the reader at first glance, Anderson describes them thoroughly throughout the text, using language accessible to the general public.

NOTES

1   Benedict Anderson, *Imagined Communities* (London and New York: Verso, 2006), 6.

MODULE 6
SECONDARY IDEAS

KEY POINTS

- The most important secondary theme in *Imagined Communities* is how language and images together foster collective, national consciousnesses—"imagined communities."

- In addition to presenting the modern nation as a kind of broadened single community, Anderson also looks at places where state and sub-state nationalism* clash, at nationalist sentiment that crosses official national borders, and at the role of more advanced media in contemporary national consciousness.

- All of these secondary themes contribute to Anderson's broader argument that the spread of rational European Enlightenment* ideas concerning matters such as individual liberty through texts printed in common languages created a sense of nationhood and nationalism in the Americas.

Other Ideas

Within the broader narrative of nations as "imagined communities," in *Imagined Communities* Benedict Anderson addresses some of the complexities that arise in the creation of nations and the evolution of nationalism. Following his discussion of "creole"* independence movements in the Americas (here meaning independence movements instigated by settlers with European roots), he goes on to describe the revolutions that arose in different geographical contexts after World War II,* and explores the reasons why these have been mostly framed in terms of ethnicity, nationalism, and national heroes rather than class struggle.

❝ [The nation] is imagined as a community, because, regardless of the actual inequality and exploitation that may prevail in each, the nation is always conceived as a deep, horizontal comradeship. Ultimately it is this fraternity that makes it possible, over the last two centuries, for so many millions of people, not so much to kill, as willingly die for such limited imaginings. **❞**

Benedict Anderson, *Imagined Communities*

Another significant sub-theme Anderson addresses is the issue of state repression of sub-state nationalism. In other words, he discusses the fact that there can be different notions of nationalism within a single sovereign* state (that is, a centrally governed state that makes decisions for itself). For example, a region within a country can be a minority imagined community that competes with the majority one, as we see in the cases of Catalan nationalism in Spain or Québécois nationalism in Canada, where sub-sections of the majority population see themselves as a "nation" in their own right.

These examples link to the importance of language in fostering national consciousness and imagined communities, with Catalan nationalists preferring the local Catalonian language over Spanish, and members of the Québécois community being united by a preference for French over English. When individuals can communicate more easily with each other, they can both develop new ideas and forms of interaction and mark themselves as distinct. Anderson is particularly attentive to the way that the circulation of words and images creates different emotions within an imagined community and fosters the idea that it is heroic to sacrifice one's life for one's nation.

As well as sub-nations that develop a distinctive sense of nationalism within a wider national context, Anderson also addresses nationalism that crosses national borders, uniting individuals and communities in different countries, as in the example of nationalism in the African and Jewish diasporas* (dispersed communities of people living away from the land of their origin).

As media and avenues of distribution developed, people in widely divergent geographical locations and political contexts were able to draw influence from each other, and as new types of media emerged they were able to play different, often more sophisticated roles in fostering a sense of national community.

While other thinkers and writers have tended to frame nationalism as a negative phenomenon, Anderson's approach focuses more on its potential to unify populations in a positive, inclusive way.

Exploring the Ideas

From the outset of *Imagined Communities*, Anderson argues that "since World War II, every successful revolution has defined itself in national terms [rather than in Marxist* terms]—the People's Republic of China, the Socialist Republic of Vietnam, and so forth."[1] What is perhaps missing here is a clarification of what exactly he means by the term "revolution" in this context. Otherwise, one could argue that this assertion could be challenged by recent Marxist or leftist movements in countries such as Venezuela and Bolivia, which *were* framed by their leaders as socialist* and *were* described in terms of class struggle, and to a degree can be considered successful.

In chapters 1 and 5, Anderson alludes to state repression of sub-state nationalism. As he puts it: "many 'old nations' once thought to be fully consolidated, find themselves challenged by 'sub'-nationalisms within their borders—nationalisms that, naturally, dream of shedding this sub-ness one day."[2] This is a theme that could be analyzed in greater detail. In particular, what lessons can be drawn from competing imagined communities within multi-ethnic states such as the United Kingdom, Spain, Belgium, or Canada?

The power of language in heightening national consciousness is the major focus of chapter 3. Here Anderson cites the example of the Turkish leader Mustafa Kemal Ataturk,* who changed Turkish script from Arabic to Latin (that is, the same script used by European languages) in order to create a secular* state. Here, there is potential to engage in a deeper analysis of this specific case study and other such cases, if they exist. Furthermore, while it can be argued that Islam and the use of classical Arabic script unite many Muslims, Anderson does not directly address the ways in which competing ideas of secular nationalism might undermine transnational religious unity. This point requires further exploration in relation to Anderson's arguments regarding religion and language.

The power of personal sacrifice is identified by Anderson as a consequence of the strong emotional bond between individuals and their imagined communities. He stresses the inclusive side of nationalism, and argues that the creation of imagined communities encourages camaraderie, which, in turn, encourages people to be heroic and sacrifice themselves in war for the "common good." A compelling avenue for further study leading from this observation would be a comparison between the urge to sacrifice oneself for one's nation and the ideas that motivated sacrifice in war for other abstract or collective causes in the pre-modern era.

In chapter 6, Anderson writes about members of the same dynastic families who often ruled in different and sometimes rival states, and had no clear nationality. For example, Romanovs ruled over Tatars and Letts, Germans, Armenians, Russians, and Finns. Habsburgs ruled over Magyars, Croats, Slovaks, Italians, Ukrainians, and Austro-Germans. And Hanoverians ruled over Bengalis, Québécois, Scots, Irish, English, and the Welsh. As he puts it: "What nationality should be assigned to Bourbons ruling in France and Spain, Hohenzollerns in Prussia and Rumania, Wittelsbachs in Bavaria and Greece?"[3] It would be interesting to compare this phenomenon to transnational identities today and how this creates divided loyalties or dual allegiances, whereby one can associate oneself simultaneously with different imagined communities. Furthermore, this can be related to long-distance nationalism,* whereby a citizen who lives outside his or her country of origin might feel strongly connected to their birthplace as well as to their current home.

Anderson sees communication technology as the catalyst in all of the developments he observes, starting with the printing press.* In chapter 7, he continues this line of thought by evaluating the influence of later technological advancements, such as film, telephone, and radio, on the formation of imagined communities. Here, there is exciting potential for thinkers to apply Anderson's framework to digital media in imagined communities today.

Overlooked

In multi-ethnic states such as the United Kingdom, Canada, Belgium, and Spain, it is necessary to consider how sub-state nationalisms (sections of the population who consider themselves a "nation" in their own right) foster different, and at times competing, notions of imagined communities. For example, how do the conceptualizations of imagined communities differ between England and Scotland, between Flanders and the rest of Belgium, between Catalonia, the Basque Country, and the rest of Spain, and between Quebec and the rest of Canada? While this is an area that has been studied in detail in recent years,[4] this remains a very promising area for further research.

Anderson explores the topic of the power of sacrifice in detail, portraying this emotional imperative as a social construction of national imagined communities. Further research into the psychological and cognitive process behind individuals' willingness to surrender their lives for a perceived common cause could surely deepen our understanding of this phenomenon. For example, how did psychological factors and social pressures motivate so many Indians to fight for Britain in World War II? How can this be compared with individual sacrifice in the name of religion, such as Islam? Future studies might also consider whether it is possible to reach a point where one would be willing to sacrifice one's life for the good of an even more abstract concept, such as "Europe," another multi-nation imagined community?

Throughout the text, Anderson links print capitalism* with the emergence of nationalist sentiment. There is the potential to further analyze the evolution of other types of capitalist*-driven media, such as the telephone, the radio, the TV, the Internet, and social media, in relation to his work. How have national, sub-national, network, and even global imagined communities evolved as a result of the spread of these technologies?

NOTES

1   Benedict Anderson, *Imagined Communities* (London and New York: Verso 2006), 2.

2   Anderson, *Imagined Communities*, 3.

3   Anderson, *Imagined Communities*, 83–4.

4   For further details, see, for example, Montserrat Guibernau, *The Identity of Nations* (London: Polity, 2007); Eve Hepburn and Ricard Zapata-Barrero, eds., *The Politics of Immigration in Multi-Level States* (London: Palgrave, 2014).

MODULE 7
ACHIEVEMENT

KEY POINTS

- Anderson's placement of the origins of nationalism* in the Americas challenged well-established Eurocentric* assumptions and presented a unique modernist* understanding of the development of nations and nationalism.

- *Imagined Communities* successfully builds on the work of early and contemporary modernist scholars, and its publication enlivened debate among competing schools of thought.

- Anderson's achievement has arguably been undermined by his superficial treatment of some important themes and the fact that there is no academic consensus on the origins and evolution of nations and nationalism.

Assessing the Argument

Benedict Anderson's *Imagined Communities* was a groundbreaking text when it was first published in 1983, providing a novel, modernist understanding of the origins and evolution of nations and nationalism. Today, it remains an influential text in the social sciences, particularly in the discipline of nationalism studies.*

In his attempt to put forward a "modular"* model of nation, and with his desire to reach a broad, interdisciplinary audience, however, Anderson arguably addresses some key points in insufficient depth. For example, from a Marxist* perspective, while he does relate the material conditions of ordinary people to changes in popular consciousness, he underplays both the political and the economic drivers of European imperialism* and the complexities of class

❝ It is imagined as sovereign* because the concept was born in an age in which Enlightenment* and Revolution were destroying the legitimacy of the divinely ordained, hierarchical dynastic realm ... nations dream of being free ... The gage and emblem of this freedom is the sovereign state. ❞

Benedict Anderson, *Imagined Communities*

struggle. This relates to postcolonial* critiques—critiques, that is, that seek to address the various social, political, and cultural legacies of colonialism—made by the Palestinian American scholar Edward Said* and the Indian American political scientist Partha Chatterjee,* who argue that consciousness develops differently from one context to another because it emanates from a unique set of lived experiences and social struggles. In this regard, they argue that those who imagined new nations in the Americas did not simply seek to replicate models of nationhood based on European Enlightenment* values. Chatterjee gives the example of African nations, such as Algeria, which fought for independence, desiring to be modern but not European.[1]

The broad interdisciplinarity of the text—its debt and contribution to many different academic disciplines—will likely continue to inspire further analysis from thinkers in a range of disciplines. The subject of nations and nationalism is a highly complex one, and there is no academic consensus on their origins or evolution.

Achievement in Context

Imagined Communities made an original contribution to the modernist and constructivist* schools of thought by highlighting the link between capitalism,* printed text in common languages, and the development of nations and nationalism. Furthermore, Anderson offered great insight into religion, time, space, imagination, and emotion in relation to the Americas, which had previously been largely ignored by scholars of nationalism studies.

As a modernist and constructivist text, *Imagined Communities* added to and expanded on the work of nationalism scholars and historians such as Tom Nairn,* Eric Hobsbawm,* John Breuilly,* and others, to present a comprehensive challenge to rival schools of thought. In particular, their view opposes that of the nationalism scholar Anthony Smith,* who argues that modern nations, nationalism, and national identity stem from pre-modern sentiments, myths, and symbols. According to Smith, those states without an important pre-modern history tend to have weak or artificial nationalism. He also asserts that emotional sacrifice is connected to the generational notion of preexisting ethnic groups.[2] Anderson's emphasis in *Imagined Communities* on New World nationalism (referring to the Americas, considered in the light of European—"Old World"—colonialism) fostered by creole* elites clearly rejects the necessity of a pre-modern foundation as a condition of strong nationhood. Furthermore, Anderson, in contrast to Smith, suggests that one's willingness to die for one's nation is socially constructed through a new sense of shared identity.

Limitations

While the text's global success demonstrates its popularity among students, scholars, and non-specialist readers around the world, there are aspects of it that prevent its universal acceptance. In the afterword to his 2006 second revised edition, Anderson briefly addresses some of these aspects.

Translators have had to amend certain aspects of the text in line with their distinctive national cultures. He gives the example of the Japanese translation where English literary citations were replaced by more readily accessible Japanese ones. Censorship has also been an issue in some countries; Anderson points out the specific example of

Indonesia, where, until the fall of the regime led by the nation's second president Suharto* in 1998, no official translation of the book was allowed. This was also the case in China, where it was published but amended substantially.

In relation to multi-ethnic contexts where there are competing imagined communities because of competing definitions of nationhood—such as the Spanish nation and the distinct Catalonian sub-national identity, or Scottish nationalism within the wider British context—Anderson's model, which arguably does not consider sub-nations in sufficient detail, could benefit from further reflection and research; it is interesting that, according to the most recent edition (2006), *Imagined Communities* has been translated into the Catalan* language in Spain—but not into Spanish.

The nationalism scholar John Breuilly has argued that the sources and origins of nationalism that Anderson identified are applicable to certain geographical case studies more than others, leaving Anderson vulnerable to the accusation that he focused on the Americas and Europe, and over-generalized his findings. Breuilly asserts that the cultural idiosyncrasies and lived experiences of each geographical context are more varied and locally relevant than Anderson gives them credit for. He believes that Anderson's model works well for Latin America, British East Africa, and French Indochina (Vietnam), but questions how well it would apply to Russia or India.[3]

Another area that impedes *Imagined Communities* is the complex and varied relationship between religion and nationalism. Nationalism has long been problematic to religious purists, some of whom see a form of unity based on race, ethnicity, or geography as a barrier to the religious bond that unites them. For example, in Islam, there is the belief in the Ummah,* or Islamic community—a concept that transcends national boundaries. Although religion and nationalism have long been incompatible on the surface, many people inevitably hold strong loyalties both to their nation and to a transnational religious identity. With the rare exception of fundamentalists (such as the radical militant organization sometimes known as Islamic State,* or Da'esh) who demand that people discard national identity and avow only their religious identity, many people around the world can reconcile living with both national and transnational religious identity. It is possible and common, for example, for one to identify as Kuwaiti, Arab, and Muslim, or British, Irish, and Catholic,* simultaneously relating to three separate but interwoven imagined communities.

NOTES

1   For further details, see: Partha Chatterjee, *Nationalist Thought and the Colonial World* (London: Zed Books, 1986); Edward Said, *Culture and Imperialism* (New York: Vintage Books, 1993).

2   John Hutchinson and Anthony Smith, *EthniCity* (Oxford: Oxford University Press, 1996).

3   John Breuilly, "Approaches to Nationalism," in Gopal Balakrishnan, ed., *Mapping the Nation*, 146–74 (London: Verso, 1996).

MODULE 8
PLACE IN THE AUTHOR'S WORK

KEY POINTS

- A scholar of nations and nationalism,* Benedict Anderson has primarily focused in his previous work on Southeast Asian politics and culture, with a particular emphasis on Indonesia.

- *Imagined Communities* is the author's most respected academic contribution. It positioned him as a leading scholar of nationalism studies* and an internationally renowned social scientist.

- Since 1983, the text has been an important reference point in nationalism studies, and one of the most cited texts in the humanities and social sciences.

Positioning

Prior to *Imagined Communities*, Benedict Anderson had never published comparably groundbreaking research on nationalism, and was yet to arrive at his current status as a renowned academic. In the United States, he was a central figure in Cornell University's Modern Indonesian Studies program and an expert on Southeast Asian politics and culture, a subject he had written on extensively since 1959.

Anderson wrote *Imagined Communities* at the age of 45, and the text clearly reflects the intellect of a mature academic. It incorporates theory, references to the key global events of the times, and his lived experiences in places such as Ireland, the United Kingdom, and Indonesia. In it, he identifies himself as an interdisciplinarian, a Marxist,* a member of the progressive New Left* of the 1960s and 1970s, a historical materialist,* and a modernist* and constructivist* with regard to his theoretical approach to nationalism.

❝ Well, it's a book I wrote when I was 45. That's nearly 25 years ago. I have a relationship to that book as to a daughter who has grown up and run off with a bus driver: I see her occasionally but, really, she has gone her own merry way. I can wish her good luck, but now she belongs with someone else. What would I change in the book? Well, should I try to change my daughter? **❞**

Benedict Anderson, in Lorenz Khazaleh, "Interview with Benedict Anderson: I Like Nationalism's Utopian Elements"

Since the publication of *Imagined Communities* in 1983, Anderson has been a key reference point in nationalism studies and beyond, to the point where he is arguably as well-known as, or perhaps even better known than, his brother Perry Anderson,* an esteemed social scientist at the University of California, Los Angeles and a leading figure of the New Left. In this regard, *Imagined Communities* must be seen as the most important text in the author's body of work, though he has made many other significant contributions.

Integration

While *Imagined Communities* launched Anderson into superstardom in the academic world, it should not be seen as a stand-alone career project. Prior to 1983, he had published extensive research on language, culture, religion, power, revolution, and nationalism in Indonesia,[2] all of which helped shape his outlook in the text to some extent. Furthermore, following the publication of *Imagined Communities*, Anderson has continued to author significant works on these themes, such as his introduction to the consciousness scholar Gopal Balakrishan's* *Mapping the Nation* (1996), as well as *The Spectre of Comparisons: Nationalism, Southeast Asia and the World* (1998) and *Under Three Flags: Anarchism and the Anti-colonial Imagination* (2005).

Anderson's vision towards nationalism remained relatively consistent from 1983 to 1991, the year he published his first revised edition of *Imagined Communities*. Since then, however, it has changed significantly. Whereas he had previously defended the enduring relevance of nations and nationalism in a globalizing* world (a world in which economic, political, and cultural ties across continents are becoming ever closer), in his introduction to *Mapping the Nation* (1996) he asserted the contrary, claiming that globalization was rupturing the "hyphen that for two hundred years yoked state and nation."[3] He argued that new fragile nation-states were emerging in the former Soviet Union,* Eastern Europe, and sub-Saharan Africa; and even in strong nation-states portable identities were calling into question citizens' allegiance. He also claimed that the growing trend towards the elimination of compulsory military service in Europe was partially responsible for the erosion of nation-state building and nationalism, and global concerns over common issues of concern were now requiring global collaboration.

Significance

While *Imagined Communities* remains one of the 35 most cited texts in the social sciences[4] and has reached a large interdisciplinary audience,[5] some scholars such as Partha Chatterjee* have viewed Anderson's pre- and post-1991 vision on nations and nationalism as problematically inconsistent. Although this shift in Anderson's position clearly came in response to post-Cold War* developments related to nation-state formation, globalization, and nationalism, as well as in response to criticism of his work, his reasoning today is still not entirely clear. In 2006, when Anderson published his second and last revised edition of *Imagined Communities*, he had a perfect opportunity to reengage meaningfully in the ongoing debate. He claimed, however, that although he would like to, doing so was now beyond his present means; instead he offered only a nostalgic self-commending afterword about the trajectory of *Imagined Communities* and the great global success it has achieved since it was first published. Subsequently, he has not addressed critiques of *Imaginary Communities* any further. Since 2006, he has published just one, unrelated book: *The Fate of Rural Hell: Asceticism and Desire in Buddhist Thailand* (2012). Nevertheless, *Imagined Communities* remains a key reference point in nationalism studies and the social sciences more broadly.

The text has also found an impact outside of the academic world. As Anderson points out in the afterword of his 2006 second revised edition, *Imagined Communities* has been used as a political tool in nationalist disputes such as those between Taiwan and China, Macedonia and Greece, and Catalonia and Spain. For example, in the early 1990s, there were nationalist marches in Greece that claimed the name of Macedonia for Greece, despite the existence of a recognized nation called the Federal Republic of Macedonia. The book was translated into Greek during that period to encourage Greeks to think about the nation in an imagined rather than fixed way. And in the Chinese version, the text was altered in translation, labeling Taiwan as the "beautiful but vulgar, passionate but anti-intellectual" island.[6]

NOTES

1   Thomson Reuters, *ISI Web of Science* (New York: Thomson Reuters, 2006).

2   For further details see: Benedict Anderson, *Some Aspects of Indonesian Politics under the Japanese Occupation, 1944–1945* (Ithaca, NY: Cornell University Press, 1961); Anderson, "Indonesia: Unity Against Progress," *Current History* (1965): 75–81; Anderson, "The Cultural Factors in the Indonesian Revolution," *Asia* 20 (1970–1): 48–65; Anderson, *Java in a Time of Revolution: Occupation and Resistance, 1944–6* (Ithaca, NY: Cornell University Press, 1972); Anderson, "The Idea of Power in Javanese Culture," in Claire Holt, Benedict Anderson, and Joseph Siegel, eds., *Culture and Politics in Indonesia* (Ithaca, NY: Cornell University Press, 1972); Sujatno, "Revolution and Social Tensions in Surakarta 1945–1950," trans. Benedict Anderson, *Indonesia* 17: 99–112; Benedict Anderson, "Religion and Politics in Indonesia since Independence," in Benedict Anderson, M. Nakamura, and M. Slamet, eds., *Religion and Social Ethos in Indonesia* (Melbourne: Monash University, 1977), 21–32.

3 Benedict Anderson, "Introduction," in Gopal Balakrishnan, ed., *Mapping the Nation*, 1–16 (London: Verso, 1996).

4 Thomson Reuters, *ISI Web of Science* (New York: Thomson Reuters, 2006).

5 Benedict Anderson, *Imagined Communities* (London and New York: Verso, 2006).

6 Anderson, *Imagined Communities*, 207.

SECTION 3
IMPACT

MODULE 9
THE FIRST RESPONSES

KEY POINTS

- *Imagined Communities* offered a novel, modernist* perspective on nations and nationalism;* since publication, it has been an important point of reference in nationalism studies* and in other disciplines.

- The nationalism scholar Anthony Smith* has made the most prominent challenge to Anderson, arguing that nations and nationalism are not wholly modern creations, but rather stem from pre-modern conditions.

- Anderson has defended his modernist stance against criticism from Smith and others, and addresses these critiques in later editions of *Imagined Communities*.

Criticism

Benedict Anderson's *Imagined Communities* has received criticism from different angles. At present, there remains no consensus on the definition of nationalism, its sources and origins, or its fundamental concepts. The modernist field remains divided on what periods and aspects of modernity are most relevant, and they are continually challenged by ethno-symbolists,* such as Anthony Smith, Patrick Geary,* and John Armstrong.* These thinkers do not deny the modernity of nations and nationalism, but argue that these concepts cannot be comprehensively understood without accounting for pre-modern conditions.

Smith has put forth the most prominent critique of *Imagined Communities*. He argues that "we cannot derive the identity, the location or even the character of the units that we term nations from the processes of modernization *tout court* [i.e. and nothing else] … We

> ❝ Anderson is entirely correct in his suggestion
> that it is 'print-capitalism'* which provides the new
> institutional space for the development of the 'modern'
> national language. However, the specificities of the
> colonial situation do not allow a simple transposition of
> European patterns of development. ❞
>
> Partha Chatterjee, *The Nation and Its Fragments*

must go further back and look at the pre-modern social and cultural antecedents and contexts of these emergent nations to explain why these and not other communities and territories became nations and why they emerged when they did."[1]

Postcolonial* scholars, who address the cultural and political legacies of colonialism, have also been critical. The historian and political scientist Partha Chatterjee* in particular argues that Anderson's definition of imagined community fails to show an in-depth understanding of the complexities of European colonialism* in Africa and Asia.[2] From his viewpoint, colonies had national institutional structures imposed on them by the West. As a result, following independence, they inevitably followed European paths and reproduced European assumptions, practices, and discussions relating to the exercise of power.[3] Yet, at the same time, he argues that in the pursuit of independence, each colonized* nation develops its own spiritual nationalism, which is not simply a mirror image of the colonizer. The essence of Chatterjee's critique is that Anderson's model is presented as a generalization, which works well in the examples Anderson provides but does not hold up elsewhere.

Responses

In 1991, Benedict Anderson authored a revised edition of *Imagined Communities* that included his first formal response to criticisms of the work. In it, he added a new chapter entitled "Census, Map, Museum"[4] in response to Chatterjee's persuasive critique in *Nationalist Thought and the Colonial World: A Derivative Discourse?* (1986), and to address the shortcomings highlighted by the Thai historian Thongchai Winichakul* in *Siam Mapped: A History of the Geo-Body of Siam* (1988).

Anderson addresses these critiques directly and takes the opportunity to amend his position with humility: "My short-sighted assumption then [in 1983] was that official nationalism in the colonized worlds of Asia and Africa was modeled directly on that of the dynastic states of nineteenth century Europe. Subsequent reflection has persuaded me that this view was hasty and superficial, and that the immediate genealogy should be traced to the imaginings of the colonial state."[5]

He then explains that three elements—the census, the map, and the museum—transformed the way the colonies imagined their domination. According to Anderson, censuses established institutional ethno-racial classifications so that colonial governments could categorize and quantify populations for the purpose of exploitation. Maps made vast, abstract spaces and arbitrary boundaries easier to grasp through visual representation. People could now easily see where their nation began and ended. At the same time, maps facilitated and justified exploration, control, and colonial expansion. Once drafted, they were replicated in magazines, on tablecloths, on hotel walls, and in other noticeable places, with the aim of penetrating the popular imagination. Anderson thanks Winichakul for bringing this point to his attention through his analysis of nationhood in nineteenth-century Siam, as Thailand was then known. Finally, Anderson adds, monuments and museums are an important tool of nationalism to construct and uphold visual images of the colonizer and the colonized.

Conflict and Consensus
Benedict Anderson's modernist, constructivist* vision of the sources and origins of nationalism has received much praise and criticism since

publication. Within the modernist and postmodernist* schools, which differ in terms of whether nationalism is seen to be based on "real" nations or on constructed identity, most scholars have praised him for his original contributions while simultaneously disagreeing with some aspects of his research. Debate continues, for example, over when the modern period can be said to start, which conditions of modernity should draw the most focus, and how globalization* continues to change contemporary concepts of nationalism.

The influential sociologist Ernest Gellner,* for example, identifies nations and nationalism as products of the transition from an agricultural society to an industrial one rather than as resulting from print capitalism; and the Marxist* historian Eric Hobsbawm* argued that national movements create nations by inventing the notion of shared traditions through the objects associated with these movements, such as flags, national anthems, celebrations, and folk costumes. Following the end of the long period of tension between the United States and the Soviet Union* known as the Cold War* (1946–91), Hobsbawm also questioned how much nationalism still mattered in an age of globalization; with ever-increasing movement and activity across borders, Hobsbawm saw that nations and nationalism had become less important, and he believed that this trend would likely continue in the future.

Praise and critique have also come from ethno-symbolists, of whom Anthony Smith is the best known. While commending Anderson for his work and highlighting his important contribution to nationalism studies, Smith emphasized that nations and nationalism cannot be understood adequately without accounting for pre-modern ethnic consciousness, myths, and symbols.

Since the end of the Cold War, the field of nationalism studies has been open to new critiques, which have focused on its relevance in a globalized, interdependent world. Significant events in the late twentieth and early twenty-first century might demand completely new ways of thinking within this field. The collapse of the Soviet Union in 1991; Russia's fall from superpower status and later reemergence; ethnic conflict in places such as Iraq, the former Yugoslavia,* and Rwanda; the economic rise of Japan, China, India, and Brazil to more powerful positions to challenge American political and economic dominance; global terrorism and the sometimes dubious government responses to it following the terrorist attacks of September 11, 2001 ("9/11")*; advances in media and transport; immigration and multiculturalism; and sub-state independence movements in places such as Quebec, Scotland, and Catalonia—all these have added new angles to existing debates.

NOTES

1   Anthony Smith, *The Nation in History: Historiographical Debates about Ethnicity and Nationalism* (Hanover, NH: University Press of New England, 2000), 69–70.

2   See: Partha Chatterjee, *Nationalist Thought and the Colonial World* (London: Zed Books, 1986); Chatterjee, *The Nation and its Fragments: Colonial and Postcolonial Histories* (Princeton, NJ: Princeton University Press, 1993).

3   Chatterjee, *The Nation and its Fragments*, 5.

4   Benedict Anderson, *Imagined Communities* (London and New York: Verso, 2006), XIV.

5   Anderson, *Imagined Communities*, 167.

MODULE 10
THE EVOLVING DEBATE

KEY POINTS

- *Imagined Communities* is a key reference point in nationalism studies* and the social sciences more broadly.

- The text is an important work from the modernist* school of nationalism studies. This contrasts with scholars who argue that nations and nationalism are natural or stem from pre-modern conditions.

- Since its publication, there has been a much stronger emphasis on the ways in which different forms of technology and media shape nationalism and ideas of nationhood.

Uses and Problems

Benedict Anderson's *Imagined Communities* has encouraged three decades of debate across academic disciplines, and much scholarship on nations and nationalism. It has contributed to the broader school of thought known as modernism, which emphasizes political, economic, social, and cultural transformations from the sixteenth century onwards, and has presented a formidable challenge to the once-dominant belief that nations are natural and have existed since time immemorial.

Since the publication of *Imagined Communities*, scholars such as Anatoliy Gruzd* have put a much stronger emphasis on the political and social construction of nations and nationalism in the modern era through mass media and social networking. For example, political discourse analysis*—the analysis of oral and written communication to explain policy processes, outcomes, and directions—has become a prolific subfield of study in the social sciences.

❝ I must be the only one writing about nationalism*
who doesn't think it ugly. If you think about researchers
such as Gellner* and Hobsbawm,* they have quite
a hostile attitude to nationalism. I actually think that
nationalism can be an attractive ideology. I like its
Utopian* elements. ❞

Benedict Anderson, in Lorenz Khazaleh, "Interview with Benedict Anderson:
I Like Nationalism's Utopian Elements"

As a result of the constructive dialogue between Benedict
Anderson and scholars such as Eric Hobsbawm,* Anthony Smith,*
Partha Chatterjee,* John Breuilly,* and other historians, social
scientists, and scholars of nationalism, theorists across the field broadly
agree that each national context and its unique, historical lived
experiences must be accounted for and cannot be generalized using a
universal model; the general model of imagined communities as
originally put forth by Anderson is one such. It should be noted,
however, that there is still no scholarly consensus regarding the specific
origins, sources, and evolution of nationalism, and how precisely it can
be defined.

Schools of Thought

Imagined Communities focuses on the evolution of print capitalism*
from the beginning of the sixteenth century onwards, and identifies
this as the catalyst for developing nationhood and nationalism.
Nationalism studies scholars working today all have a common
starting point in the work by the first important historians of
nationalism, the American thinkers Hans Kohn* and Carlton Hayes,*
who constructed the concepts of "good" and "bad" nationalism and
traced their evolution over time.

The modernist school of nationalism studies is, of course, characterized by a shared view of nation as a product of the modern era, but even here there is a diversity of opinion regarding exactly when modernity begins. For the British historian Elie Kedourie,* it is the French Revolution* of 1789–99 and the birth of the centralized French state; for Anderson, it is the development of print capitalism following the invention of the printing press;* for the social scientist Ernest Gellner,* it is the development of infrastructure and the movement of people associated with the transition from an agricultural to an industrial economy. Another increasingly prominent debate centers on the extent to which nationalism matters in a globalized* world.

Ethno-symbolists* such as Anthony Smith, in contrast, link modern symbols, myths, values, customs, and traditions to pre-modern conditions and identities. Although Smith has been the greatest critic of the modernist school, even he agrees that modernization was the force that shifted ancient communities into nations.

The interdisciplinary nature of *Imagined Communities* has also motivated critiques from other fields, the most notable of which have come from postcolonial* scholars, such as Chatterjee and Edward Said.* They were drawn to comment on Anderson's work because they felt it neglected to account adequately for the different anticolonial* and postcolonial experiences of African and Asian nations.

In Current Scholarship

Anderson, Hobsbawm, Gellner, Chatterjee, Breuilly, and Tom Nairn* have all had a strong mutual influence, encouraging reflection of each other's scholarship. Several texts influenced *Imagined Communities*, including Gellner's *Thought and Change* (1964), Nairn's *The Break-up of Britain* (1977), and Hobsbawm's "Some Reflections on 'The Break-up of Britain'" (1977). And Anderson's revised editions were influenced by critiques from the aforementioned scholars and others.

In nationalism studies, Anderson has motivated subsequent research from modernists, postmodernists, and ethno-symbolists, and at a more general level, the book has been very influential among historians, political scientists, anthropologists, and postcolonial theorists.

Regarding specific students of Anderson, in his second revised edition, published in 2006, he mentions a few, including Takashi Shiraishi* and Saya Shiraishi,* who produced the text's first translation in Japanese to pedagogically challenge Japanese insularity (that is, its inward-looking nature), and the Croatian sociologist and lecturer at the University of Ljubljana Silva Meznaric,* who attempted to publish a Serbo-Croat translation prior to the fall of Yugoslavia* in order to fight against Croatian and Serbian nationalist myths.

A number of Anderson's former students and colleagues have aided him in translating his work around the world, facilitating an increased global awareness of *Imagined Communities*.

MODULE 11
IMPACT AND INFLUENCE TODAY

KEY POINTS

- Although *Imagined Communities* has received criticism from different disciplines, its overall importance as a groundbreaking text has only rarely been questioned.

- The main challenges to the text have come from proponents of ethno-symbolism,* who argue that nations and nationalism* stem from pre-modern conditions, and from postcolonial* scholars, who argue that each geographical context is based on unique lived experiences and social struggles.

- Modernists* continue to emphasize, in contrast to their rivals, that nations and nationalism are modern creations that evolved alongside the development of the economic and social system of capitalism*.

Position

Benedict Anderson's *Imagined Communities* has been praised and critiqued by other modernists and by thinkers from rival schools of thought in nationalism studies,* and has received criticism from outside its immediate discipline. Its overall importance as a seminal text is, however, widely accepted. Upon publication in 1983, the text (surprisingly, perhaps) provoked no formal response from the influential sociologist Ernest Gellner,* who was arguably the most respected scholar on the subject at the time. In contrast, it has been scrutinized to a considerable extent by fellow modernists Eric Hobsbawm* and John Breuilly,* and the ethno–symbolist Anthony Smith.* All of these scholars built on the previous research of key figures such as the British historian and nationalism scholar Elie

> 66 The nation is imagined as limited because even the largest of them, encompassing perhaps a billion living human beings, has finite, if elastic, boundaries, beyond which lie other nations. 99

Benedict Anderson, *Imagined Communities*

Kedourie,* the Scottish nationalism scholar Tom Nairn,* the British political scientist Hugh Seton-Watson,* and the Czech American sociologist Karl Deutsch.*

Today, *Imagined Communities* is one of the key reference points in nationalism studies. It constitutes an important part of the modernist school of thought, in contrast to primordialism* and ethno-symbolism. It is also of the Marxist* tradition in that it represents nations and nationalism as social constructions that have developed in conjunction with capitalism.

Interaction

Imagined Communities remains a foundational text for students and scholars of the social sciences. It addresses the modern social construction of nations and nationalism and their link to economics, technology, the media, and class struggle. Today, the text continues to challenge existing ideas insofar as it is an important part of the modernist, constructivist* view in nationalism studies (according to which nationalism is a recent phenomenon, and derived from social processes). It also remains significant to current debates on the relevance of nations in a globalized* world, as well as on the power of technology and media discourse in relation to imperialism,* social movements, and the construction of different imagined communities.

Today, debate in nationalism studies around the origins and sources of nationalism is relatively stale. There are now two prominent positions: modernism and ethno-symbolism. Modernists reject the idea that nations have existed since the dawn of civilization, instead viewing nationalism purely as a product of modernization that has evolved alongside capitalism. This is the viewpoint that has been taken up by scholars such as Anderson and Gellner. Within this school, however, there are important variants, such as John Breuilly's focus on the role of political institutions and geopolitics* (the study of how political and economic geography shapes politics and international relations) in evoking nationalism, and Eric Hobsbawm's emphasis on invented customs and traditions.

The main opposing perspective at present is ethno-symbolism, a school of thought that links modern symbols, myths, values, and traditions to pre-modern conditions. Its most recognized proponent is Anthony Smith. This school has evolved as a compromise between the primordialists and perennialists* of yesteryear, and the wave of convincing modernist literature published since Kedourie's *Nationalism* (1960), which highlighted the French Revolution* and the birth of the centralized French state as the emblematic events of modernity.

The Continuing Debate

Since writing the introduction to *Mapping the Nation* (1996), a collection of papers edited by the scholar Gopal Balakrishnan,* Anderson has largely withdrawn from the debate within nationalism studies. His unwillingness to engage with it is evident in the second, and most recent, revised edition of 2006, in which he merely traces the trajectory and success of his book since 1983, without offering deeper insight into how nationalism has evolved. He claimed that expanding on the arguments presented in earlier editions of *Imagined Communities* was beyond his present means. While *Imagined Communities* remains a foundational text in the study of nations and nationalism, Anderson is no longer an active participant in that debate.

Since the collapse in the 1990s of the Soviet Union* and the communist state of Yugoslavia* (the former republic is now the separate states of Slovenia, Croatia, Bosnia and Herzegovina, Macedonia, Serbia, and Montenegro), the sheer volume of literature on nationalism has rocketed. However, as the political science professor Walker Connor* has pointed out, a lack of consensus on the definition of nationalism, its origins, and its fundamental concepts has retarded progress in the field.[1]

Many key modernist scholars such as Hobsbawm, Gellner, and Kedourie are now deceased, and the current modernist school remains split into those who emphasize nationalism as an ideology (as is the case when politicians use nationalism as a tool to unite some at the expense of others) and those who emphasize it as a positive cultural phenomenon. The start date and evolution of modernity are also areas of contention. Finally, scholars across all schools of thought are divided by the degree to which they believe nations and nationalism still matter in a globalized, post-Cold War* world.

Imagined Communities is likely to remain a significant interdisciplinary seminal text in the social sciences. It provides a novel, modernist understanding of the origin and development of nations and nationalism by linking them to the decline of religion, the introduction of print capitalism,* and the interplay between nationalisms in the Americas and Europe. It also addresses the failure of Marxist* analysis to consider nationalism as a force that unites as well as divides people.

The text can be considered, finally, as having made an important contribution to the broader modernist school of thought.

NOTES

1   See Walker Connor, *Ethno-nationalism: The Quest for Understanding* (Princeton, NJ: Princeton University Press, 2004).

MODULE 12
WHERE NEXT?

KEY POINTS

- The lack of consensus over the definition of nationalism,* its sources and origins, and its fundamental concepts, will continue to encourage further research and debate.

- *Imagined Communities* will likely continue to be a key reference point for scholars of nationalism studies.*

- The interdisciplinary nature of the text will also likely make it a well-used resource in a range of fields in the social sciences from political science to postcolonial* studies to media studies.

Potential

Benedict Anderson's *Imagined Communities* is likely to remain one of the principal points of reference and departure for modernists* and constructivists* in the field of nationalism studies. This is true because the divide separating modernists from rival schools of thought will not be immediately resolved. Even within the modernist school, there will continue to be differing viewpoints over which period and which conditions of modernity are most relevant to nationalism. Diversity of opinion over the definition of nationalism, its sources and origins, and its fundamental concepts will continue to encourage debate and further study. Finally, due to its interdisciplinary focus, it is likely to remain relevant to a wide array of disciplines beyond the confines of nationalism studies. These range from political science to postcolonial theory to religious and media studies.

A number of the main themes of *Imagined Communities* seem ripe for exploration by the next generation of nationalism scholars,

❝ This is a splendid book to read—engaging, imaginative, sweeping, relevant, humane. It should be put in the hands of students, for despite the array of learning, it never wraps up an argument but challenges and provokes to further questions. **❞**

Anthony Reid, "Reviewed Work: *Imagined Communities. Reflections on the Origin and Spread of Nationalism* by Benedict Anderson"

including culture, print capitalism,* nationalism in the developing world, American Studies, social movements and structures, and the national imagination. It is easy to see the potential for Anderson's text to be applied to further research on topics such as: media; identity; transnationalism ("national" identity that extends beyond state borders); hybridity* (the idea that in a multicultural society, there is a continual exchange of culture between different groups, and a continual negotiation of power and identity); multi-ethnic states; failed states; postcolonial nationalism (nationalism that exists in formerly colonized* nations); cultural expression through art, music, film, and literature; social movements; and network societies* (social, political, economic, and cultural changes that result from digital information and communications technologies).

Future Directions

Drawing on the aims and methods of many academic disciplines, and appealing to a general audience, *Imagined Communities* offers something to many fields beyond nationalism studies. As a frequently cited text in the humanities,[1] it has helped advance debates on issues such as: European colonial racism in the Americas; social movements as a form of resistance to imperialism;* the link between technology and capitalism;* the relationship between religion and nationalism; the importance of social construction (a society's capacity to build the "structures" and consensus that define it); and the power of language, imagination, and emotion.

One particularly promising area for future exploration is the rise of imagined communities through social media. The mobilization of different causes through platforms such as Facebook and Twitter will likely attract more and more scholarly interest in the coming years.

Imagined Communities will also continue to prove useful for thinkers who disagree with elements of Anderson's argumentation, taking it as a useful scholarly point of departure. For example, religious scholars have challenged Anderson's position on the decline of religion as a central ingredient in the modern nation, arguing that Muslim nations are to some degree united by Islam and classical Arabic script.

Summary

Imagined Communities begins by tracing the decline of religion, European dynastic powers, and Latin as a privileged language after 1500, a year Anderson takes as the start of the modern era. It then focuses on the emergence of print capitalism after the invention of the printing press* which made printed material—specifically newspapers and novels—affordable to ordinary people for the first time. This also meant that this material had to be printed in the vernacular languages used by these new consumers of books. All of this revolutionized communication and the exchange of ideas, and meant that ordinary people could engage with the ideas of the European Enlightenment.*

At the end of the eighteenth century, creole* elites (that is, landowners, small merchants, military men, and functionaries)* within European colonies in the Americas developed a sense of nation inspired by Enlightenment philosophy and in reaction to the discrimination and oppression they experienced at the hands of the colonial rulers. Their nationalism then became "modular,"* meaning that it could be applied, with varying degrees of self-consciousness, to other political and social contexts. The "imagined community"—

which Anderson defines as an "imagined, inherently limited and sovereign* political community" in which "members of even the smallest nation will never know most of their fellow members, meet, or even hear of them, yet in the minds of each lives the image of their communion"[2]—became necessary in a secular* world without religion to provide an authoritative sense of a definitive beginning and end.

These parallel developments yielded the modern nation and nationalism, and, as Anderson observes, these concepts inspire such a strong emotional bond to one's nation and the people to whom one feels connected by national citizenship, that some are even willing to sacrifice their lives for the "common good."

This vision of nation and nationalism is "modernist" in that it portrays nationalism as a historical and constructed phenomenon of the modern era, rather than a concept as old as civilization itself. Moreover, by linking print capitalism to culture, language, and nationalism, Anderson claims to address what he perceives as a shortcoming of Marxist* theory, which he claims fails to explain why in the post-World War II* era "socialist"* revolutions were waged through a vision of nationalism and national heroes and not class struggle. Finally, by placing the origins of nations and nationalism in the Americas rather than Europe, Anderson importantly challenges the often Eurocentric* nature of many scholarly fields, including nationalism studies, in a kind of reorientation that many consider an essential feature of contemporary thought.

NOTES

1   Thomson Reuters, *ISI Web of Science* (New York: Thomson Reuters, 2007).

2   Benedict Anderson, *Imagined Communities* (London and New York: Verso, 2006), 207.

GLOSSARY

GLOSSARY OF TERMS

Anarchism: a political philosophy that argues for no government and for society to be organized on a voluntary, cooperative basis.

Anticolonial: this term refers to the struggle of the European colonies in Africa, Asia, and the Americas against European colonial powers.

Aristocracy: a system of government in which power is held by the nobility and continues through hereditary succession.

Bourgeois nationalism: in Marxist theory, this is the deliberate attempt of the ruling classes to divide people based on nationality in order to disrupt the unity of the working class. The "bourgeoisie" refers to the ruling classes or those who own the means of production. This contrasts with workers, who sell their labor power, from which property owners make a profit.

Capitalism: an economic system based on private ownership, private enterprise, and the maximization of profit.

Catalan: the language spoken in the region of Spain known as Catalonia, of which Barcelona is the capital.

Catholic: relating to the Roman Catholic Church (one of the two major branches of the Christian religion, the other being Protestantism).

Classical Marxism: the political and economic theory as laid out by Karl Marx and Friedrich Engels, in contrast to Marxist ideas that more modern theorists have expounded.

Cold War: usually dated from 1947 until 1991, this was a period of military "tension" between the United States and the Soviet Union. While the two countries never engaged in direct military conflict, they engaged in covert and proxy wars and espionage against one another.

Colonialism: the policy of settling another country in order to control it politically. The European colonial period ran from the sixteenth century to the mid-twentieth century.

Colonized: the subjects of colonial rule.

Constructivism: the belief that nations and nationalism are social constructions of the modern era—that is, that they did not develop naturally, but were invented by people.

Creole: settler populations in the Americas with European roots who, influenced by Enlightenment ideas once accessible in affordable books printed in everyday language, developed a sense of nationhood in response to their unfair treatment by European imperial powers.

Decolonization: the process by which European colonies became more autonomous or independent.

Devolution: the process of transferring power from the central government of a sovereign state to sub-national governments.

Diasporas: groups that have been dispersed outside their traditional homeland, particularly involuntarily. They also sometimes include the descendants of those groups.

Dynasty: a succession of rulers from the same family or line of descent.

Enlightenment: also known as "the Age of Reason," this was a Western intellectual movement of the late seventeenth and eighteenth centuries that aimed to question tradition and religious belief while advancing knowledge of the world through the scientific method.

Ethno-nationalism: the desire of an ethnic community to have complete control over its political, economic, and social affairs.

Ethno-symbolism: the belief that modern nations and nationalism stem from pre-modern conditions.

Eton College: a private boarding school for boys in England, often considered to be one of the most elitist seats of learning in Britain.

Eurocentric: focusing on Europe to the exclusion of a broader view of the world.

Free market: An economic system in which buyers and sellers do business with little or no government intervention.

French Revolution (1789–99): a period of profound political and social transformation in France which saw the overthrow of the monarchy and the beginning of the French Republic; it influenced the course of Western history as a whole.

Functionaries: people who perform official duties, normally with a government.

Geopolitics: the study of how political and economic geography shapes politics and international relations.

Globalization: a process of international integration. Such integration takes many forms, including economic, political, and cultural.

Historical materialism: the study of political, social, and cultural transformations in relation to economics and class struggle.

Hybridity: the idea that in a multicultural society, there is a continual exchange of culture between different groups, and a continual negotiation of power and identity.

Imperialism: the policy and political consequences of one country exercising control over another, through territorial acquisition or political and economic dominance.

Industrial capitalism: an economic system in which factory owners profit from wage labor.

Industrialization: the process by which a society and an economy founded on agriculture move to a society and economy based on mechanized industry.

Institutional analysis: a methodological approach in the social sciences that focuses on structures and mechanisms that influence social order.

Iranian Revolution: the revolution in Iran in 1978–9 that overthrew the Western-backed Shah and created an Islamic Republic under Ayatollah Khomeini.

Islamic Republic: the classification given to several states that are ruled by Islamic law.

Islamic State: also known as ISIS, ISIL, and Da'esh, this is a radical Sunni Islamist militant group that currently controls parts of Syria and Iraq.

Liberalism: Despite the variation among the strands of thought integrated into the liberal tradition, from a political point of view all advocates of liberalism share the idea that politics should be concerned with protecting and enhancing individual freedom.

Long-distance nationalism: Anderson uses this term to refer to nationalistic communities who live outside the nation-state in question. For example, Israeli communities who live abroad often have strong nationalistic sentiments regarding what occurs in Israel.

Marxism: the name ascribed to the political system advocated by Karl Marx. It emphasized an end to capitalism by taking control of the means of production from individuals and placing it firmly in the hands of a central government run in the interests of ordinary working people.

Means of production: those things such as land, natural resources, and technology that are necessary for the production of goods.

Modernist: In the field of nationalist studies, modernists reject the view that nations are "natural" and date back to the beginning of time, and the perspective of ethno-symbolists that modern nations and nationalism stem from the pre-modern era—roughly, about 1500. Instead, they view the nation as a political and social creation that evolved alongside capitalism from the sixteenth century onwards.

Modular: a model that is applicable across different contexts.

Nationalism: devotion to the interests of a particular nation-state or the belief that national identity can and should be defined politically.

Nationalism studies: the interdisciplinary subfield of the social sciences that addresses the origins and development of nations and nationalism.

Network society: social, political, economic, and cultural changes that result from digital information and communications technologies.

New Left: a social and political movement that emerged in the 1960s and 1970s and sought progressive reforms.

New Left Review: a bi-monthly publication founded in 1960 covering world politics, economics, and culture.

9/11: the terrorist attacks by politically radicalized Muslim fundamentalists in the United States on September 11, 2001.

Orthodoxy: a way of thinking or a practice that is commonly accepted as standard or true.

Perennialism: a theory that differs slightly from primordialism; its proponents believe that the nation dates back to time immemorial; however, they do not necessarily believe that nations are natural—that is, based on socio-biological origins.

Political discourse analysis: the analysis of oral and written communication to explain policy processes, outcomes, and directions.

Postcolonialism: the study of the relationship between European colonial powers and their colonies, and of colonial populations since they gained independence.

Postmodernism: in nationalism studies, this is a strand of thought that argues that nationalism is not based on real nations but on constructed identity. It focuses on the importance of discourse, narratives, and invented traditions.

Primordialism: the belief that nations are natural and have existed since the beginning of time.

Print capitalism: a concept, introduced by Anderson, used to describe the conditions under which imagined communities ("nations") became possible. Anderson argues that this occurred only after the introduction of printing in vernacular languages (replacing the predominance of Latin), beginning in the early sixteenth century, which in turn united different local dialects and created common languages and discourses.

Printing press: a printing system invented by Johannes Gutenberg in 1440 that facilitated the mass production of books and other printed material.

Rationalism: a mode of thinking that emerged from the Enlightenment that stresses reason and empirical study.

Secularism: this consists of two principles: the separation of the Church and the State; and the idea that people of different religions and beliefs are equal under the law.

Shah: the title of the former monarch of Iran, who was ousted in the 1978–9 Iranian Revolution.

Socialism: the belief that society should be organized in such a way that the methods of production, distribution, and exchange are owned and regulated by the community as a whole, rather than by the privileged few.

Sovereign: a term describing a kind of political organization in which the central government of a state expresses supreme authority over its territory.

Soviet Union: a union of 15 communist republics in Eastern Europe and Central and North Asia that existed between 1917 and 1991.

Suez crisis: an important military conflict that took place in 1956 after the Egyptian President, Gamal Nassar, nationalized the Suez Canal, which had long been controlled by Britain. Britain and France objected and mobilized militarily, but were forced to withdraw by international pressure.

Third World: a term commonly used to refer to the underdeveloped and developing countries of Asia, Africa, and Latin America collectively.

Ummah: an Arabic word meaning "nation" or "community," referring to the sense of a shared Muslim identity.

United Irishmen's Rebellion of 1798: an uprising in Ireland in 1798 that sought parliamentary reform (universal male suffrage and Roman Catholic emancipation) and the elimination of British rule in Ireland.

Utopia: an ideally perfect political and social place or arrangement.

Vietnam War: a war between South Vietnam and North Vietnam from 1954 to 1975, and in which the United States engaged from 1960 to 1973. America's decision to enter the conflict was motivated in large part by a desire to contain the spread of communism, a political ideology that relies on the state ownership of the means of production, the collectivization of labor, and the abolition of social class. Communism was the ideology of the Soviet Union (1917–89), and existed in fundamental opposition to Western free-market capitalism during the Cold War.

World War II: a global conflict that took place between 1939 and 1945 between Germany, Italy, and Japan (the Axis powers) and Britain, the Soviet Union, the United States, and other nations (the Allies).

Yugoslavia: Yugoslavia was a republic that existed from 1918 to 1991. In 1991, four of its six constituent republics (Slovenia, Croatia, Bosnia and Herzegovina, and Macedonia) declared independence; Serbia and Montenegro did the same in 2003.

PEOPLE MENTIONED IN THE TEXT

Perry Anderson (b. 1938) is a professor of history and sociology at the University of California, Los Angeles. He is the brother of Benedict Anderson, and a former editor of the *New Left Review*.

John Armstrong (1922–2010) was professor emeritus of political science at the University of Wisconsin-Madison. In *Nations before Nationalism* (1982), he argued that nations precede nationalism and that there is a continuation between old ethnic consciousness and modern nations.

Mustafa Kemal Ataturk (1881–1938) founded the Republic of Turkey in 1923 following the disintegration of the Ottoman Empire. He is well known for making the country secular—that is, for separating the Church and State.

Erich Auerbach (1892–1957) was a German philologist and comparative scholar who worked as a professor at Yale University. His most important work was *Mimesis: The Representation of Reality in Western Literature* (1953).

Gopal Balakrishan is a professor of the history of consciousness at the University of California, Santa Cruz, and an editor at the *New Left Review*. He has published and edited a number of important texts, including editing *Mapping the Nation* (1996).

Anthony Barnett (b. 1942) is a British writer and campaigner for democracy. He was the founder of the online discussion forum "openDemocracy" and is the former editor of the *New Left Review*.

Walter Benjamin (1892–1940) was a German Jewish Marxist and intellectual of the Frankfurt School, a group of social scientists who analyzed the changes in Western capitalist societies since the classical theory of Karl Marx.

John Breuilly (b. 1946) is the chair of nationalism and ethnicity at the London School of Economics Department of Government. He is the author of *Nationalism and the State*, a modernist text that argues that nationalism should be understood as a form of politics that arises in opposition to the modern state.

Partha Chatterjee (b. 1947) is a political scientist, historian, and anthropologist, and currently a professor at Columbia University. He is also a postcolonial theorist.

Walker Connor (b. 1926) is widely considered to be one of the founders of the interdisciplinary field of nationalism studies. In his work, he emphasizes the link between ethnicity and nationalism and argues that the emotional bond of nationalism is non-rational in that it is linked to felt history rather than factual history.

Karl Deutsch (1912–92) was a Czech American social and political scientist who authored important works on nationalism. His most famous text on the subject was *Nationalism and Social Communication* (1953).

John Echols (1915–82) was a professor of linguistics and literature in the South East Asia program at Cornell University. He had an important influence on Benedict Anderson.

Friedrich Engels (1820–95) was a German businessman, political theorist, and author who co-wrote *The Communist Manifesto* with Karl Marx.

Patrick Geary (b. 1948) is an American professor at the Institute of Advanced Study at Princeton University and an expert on Western medieval history. While acknowledging that nationalist sentiment arose in the nineteenth century, he argues that the actual formation of European peoples must be seen as the continuation of a long-standing process that has been going on since Antiquity.

Ernest Gellner (1925–95) was a well-known British Czech philosopher, sociologist, and social anthropologist who authored *Nations and Nationalism* (1983), a text that claims that nationalism originated in the transition from agrarian to industrial societies.

Anatoliy Gruzd is an associate professor at the Ted Rogers School of Management at Ryerson University in Toronto, Canada. His research focuses on online communities, social media data stewardship, online social networks, social networks analysis, information visualization, and computer-mediated communication.

Carlton Hayes (1882–1964) was an American diplomat and educator and European historian. He authored significant works on nationalism, including *Essays on Nationalism* (1926).

Eric Hobsbawm (1917–2012) was a well-known British Marxist historian. In 1977, he authored an important piece in the *New Left Review* called "Some Reflections on 'The Break-up of Britain'" in which he offered a sharp critique of Tom Nairn's *The Break-up of Britain* (1977); this was a launch pad for Benedict Anderson's outlook in *Imagined Communities*.

Claire Holt (1901–70) was an expert on Indonesian culture and a lecturer at the department of Southeast Asian studies at Cornell University. She had an important influence on Benedict Anderson.

George Kahin (1918–2000) was a leading American academic on Southeast Asia. He was also a critic and activist against American involvement in the Vietnam War.

Elie Kedourie (1926–92) was a British historian and expert on nationalism in the Middle East. His *Nationalism* (1960) and *Nationalism in Asia and Africa* (1970) have been highly influential in shaping the modernist school of nationalism studies.

Hans Kohn (1891–1971) was a Jewish American philosopher and historian. He taught at City College of New York, Smith College, and Harvard University, and published significant research on nationalism.

Vladimir Lenin (1870–1924) was one of the leading revolutionaries in history. He founded the Russian Communist Party, masterminded the Bolshevik Revolution, and became the first leader of the Soviet Union.

Karl Marx (1818–83) was a German philosopher, economist, historian, and sociologist, and is widely considered one of the most influential social scientists. He is the author of *The Communist Manifesto* (with Friedrich Engels) (1848) and *Das Kapital* (1867).

Silva Meznaric (b. 1939) is an associate professor of the faculty of letters and arts, University of Ljubljana, Slovenia. She is a scholar of migration and ethnicity.

Tom Nairn (b. 1932) is a Scottish academic and scholar of nationalism studies. In 1977, he wrote *The Break-up of Britain*, in which he argued that Marxists had historically avoided the importance of nationalism in their research; this argument helped shape Benedict Anderson's thesis in *Imagined Communities*.

Daniel O'Connell (1775–1847) was an Irish politician who fought for the right of Irish Catholics to have political representation in the British Parliament.

Mohammad Reza Pahlavi (1919–80) was the Shah (or King) of Iran from 1941 until his overthrow in 1979.

Terrence Ranger (b. 1929) is a professor at the University of Oxford. He coedited *The Invention of Tradition* (1983) with Eric Hobsbawm.

Ronald Reagan (1911–2004) was president of the United States from 1981 to 1989. He was a member of the Republican Party and is widely credited in America with bringing an end to the Cold War.

Edward Said (1935–2003) was a Palestinian American literary scholar and public intellectual. He published several seminal works, the most prominent of which was *Orientalism* (1978).

Hugh Seton-Watson (1916–84) was a British historian and political scientist. He specialized in Russia and authored significant research on nationalism.

Saya Shiraishi is a professor at the Graduate School of Education of the University of Tokyo.

Takashi Shiraishi (b. 1950) has taught at the University of Tokyo and Cornell University. He is an expert on East Asian politics and international relations.

Anthony Smith (b. 1939) is professor emeritus of nationalism studies and ethnicity at the London School of Economics. He is an ethno-symbolist and the most renowned critic of the modernist school of nationalism studies.

Suharto (1921–2008) was the second president of Indonesia. He held office from 1967 to 1998.

Margaret Thatcher (1925–2013) was prime minister of the United Kingdom from 1979 to 1990. She was a member of the Conservative Party and is best known for nationalist discourse, Britain's victory in the Falklands War, market deregulation, privatization, and curtailing the power of trade unions.

Thongchai Winichakul (b. 1957) is professor of Southeast Asian history at the University of Wisconsin-Madison. He is an expert on Thai history and nationalism.

WORKS CITED

WORKS CITED

Alexander, Semyonov. "Interview with Benedict Anderson, 'We Study Empires as We Do Dinosaurs': Nations, Nationalism, and Empire in a Critical Perspective." *Ab Imperio* 3 (2003): 57–73.

Anderson, Benedict. "The Cultural Factors in the Indonesian Revolution." *Asia* 20 (1970–1): 48–65.

The Fate of Rural Hell: Asceticism and Desire in Buddhist Thailand. Calcutta: Seagull Books, 2012.

"The Idea of Power in Javanese Culture." In *Culture and Politics in Indonesia*, edited by Claire Holt, Benedict Anderson, and Joseph Siegel. Ithaca, NY: Cornell University Press, 1972.

Imagined Communities, second revised edition. London and New York: Verso, 2006.

"Indonesia: Unity Against Progress." *Current History* (1965): 75–81.

"Introduction." In *Mapping the Nation*, edited by Gopal Balakrishnan, 1–16. London: Verso, 1996.

Java in a Time of Revolution: Occupation and Resistance, 1944–6. Ithaca, NY: Cornell University Press, 1972.

Language and Power: Exploring Political Cultures in Indonesia. Ithaca, NY: Cornell University Press, 1990.

Religion and Politics in Indonesia since Independence. In *Religion and Social Ethos in Indonesia,* Benedict Anderson, M. Nakamura, and M. Slamet, 21–32. Melbourne: Monash University, 1977.

Some Aspects of Indonesian Politics under the Japanese Occupation, 1944–1945. Ithaca, NY: Cornell University Press, 1961.

The Spectre of Comparisons: Nationalism, Southeast Asia and the World. London: Verso, 1998.

Under Three Flags: Anarchism and the Anti-colonial Imagination. London: Verso, 2005.

Anderson, Benedict, Ruth McVey, and Frederick Bunnell. *A Preliminary Analysis of the October 1, 1965 Coup in Indonesia*. Ithaca, NY: Cornell University, 1971.

Armstrong, John. *Nations before Nationalism*. Chapel Hill, NC: University of North Carolina Press, 1982.

Balakrishnan, Gopal, ed. *Mapping the Nation*. London: Verso Books, 1996.

Breuilly, John. "Approaches to Nationalism." In *Mapping the Nation*, edited by Gopal Balakrishnan, 146–74. London: Verso, 1996.

Nationalism and the State. Manchester: Manchester University Press, 1982.

Chatterjee, Partha. *Nationalist Thought and the Colonial World: A Derivative Discourse?* London: Zed Books, 1986.

The Nation and its Fragments: Colonial and Postcolonial Histories. Princeton, NJ: Princeton University Press, 1993.

Connor, Walker. *Ethno-nationalism: The Quest for Understanding*. Princeton, NJ: Princeton University Press, 2004.

Gellner, Ernest. *Nations and Nationalism*. Ithaca, NY: Cornell University Press, 1983.

Thought and Change. London: Orion, 1964.

Giddens, Anthony. *The Constitution of Society: Outline of the Theory of Structuration*. Cambridge: Polity Press, 1984.

Guibernau, Montserrat. *The Identity of Nations*. London: Polity, 2007.

Hepburn, Eve, and Ricard Zapata-Barrero, eds. *The Politics of Immigration in Multi-Level States*. London: Palgrave, 2014.

Hobsbawm, Eric. *Nations and Nationalism since 1780: Programme, Myth, Reality*. Cambridge: Cambridge University Press, 1990.

"Some Reflections on 'The Break-up of Britain.'" *New Left Review* 105, no. 5 (1977): 3.

Hobsbawm, Eric, and Terrence Ranger, eds. *The Invention of Tradition*. Cambridge: Cambridge University Press, 1983.

Hutchinson, John, and Anthony Smith. *EthniCity*. Oxford: Oxford University Press, 1996.

Kedourie, Elie. *Nationalism*. London: Hutchinson, 1960.

Nationalism in Asia and Africa. New York: The World Publishing Company, 1970.

Khazaleh, Lorenz. "Interview with Benedict Anderson: I Like Nationalism's Utopian Elements." University of Norway website, May 25, 2011. Accessed October 4, 2015. https://www.uio.no/english/research/interfaculty-research-areas/culcom/news/2005/anderson.html.

Nairn, Tom. *The Break-up of Britain*. London: New Left Books, 1977.

The Break-up of Britain, second edition. London: Verso, 1981.

Reid, Anthony. "Reviewed Work: *Imagined Communities. Reflections on the Origin and Spread of Nationalism* by Benedict Anderson." *Pacific Affairs* 58, no. 3 (1985): 497–9.

Smith, Anthony. "Chosen Peoples." In *Ethnicity*, edited by John Hutchinson and Anthony Smith, 189–97. New York: Oxford University Press, 1996.

The Nation in History: Historiographical Debates about Ethnicity and Nationalism. Hanover, NH: University Press of New England, 2000.

Sujatno. "Revolution and Social Tensions in Surakarta 1945–1950." Translated by Benedict Anderson. *Indonesia* 17: 99–112.

Thomson Reuters. *ISI Web of Science*. New York: Thomson Reuters, 2007.

Winichakul, Thongchai. *Siam Mapped: A History of the Geo-Body of Siam*. Honolulu: University of Hawaii Press, 1994.

THE MACAT LIBRARY
BY DISCIPLINE

AFRICANA STUDIES

Chinua Achebe's *An Image of Africa: Racism in Conrad's Heart of Darkness*
W. E. B. Du Bois's *The Souls of Black Folk*
Zora Neale Huston's *Characteristics of Negro Expression*
Martin Luther King Jr's *Why We Can't Wait*
Toni Morrison's *Playing in the Dark: Whiteness in the American Literary Imagination*

ANTHROPOLOGY

Arjun Appadurai's *Modernity at Large: Cultural Dimensions of Globalisation*
Philippe Ariès's *Centuries of Childhood*
Franz Boas's *Race, Language and Culture*
Kim Chan & Renée Mauborgne's *Blue Ocean Strategy*
Jared Diamond's *Guns, Germs & Steel: the Fate of Human Societies*
Jared Diamond's *Collapse: How Societies Choose to Fail or Survive*
E. E. Evans-Pritchard's *Witchcraft, Oracles and Magic Among the Azande*
James Ferguson's *The Anti-Politics Machine*
Clifford Geertz's *The Interpretation of Cultures*
David Graeber's *Debt: the First 5000 Years*
Karen Ho's *Liquidated: An Ethnography of Wall Street*
Geert Hofstede's *Culture's Consequences: Comparing Values, Behaviors, Institutes and Organizations across Nations*
Claude Lévi-Strauss's *Structural Anthropology*
Jay Macleod's *Ain't No Makin' It: Aspirations and Attainment in a Low-Income Neighborhood*
Saba Mahmood's *The Politics of Piety: The Islamic Revival and the Feminist Subject*
Marcel Mauss's *The Gift*

BUSINESS

Jean Lave & Etienne Wenger's *Situated Learning*
Theodore Levitt's *Marketing Myopia*
Burton G. Malkiel's *A Random Walk Down Wall Street*
Douglas McGregor's *The Human Side of Enterprise*
Michael Porter's *Competitive Strategy: Creating and Sustaining Superior Performance*
John Kotter's *Leading Change*
C. K. Prahalad & Gary Hamel's *The Core Competence of the Corporation*

CRIMINOLOGY

Michelle Alexander's *The New Jim Crow: Mass Incarceration in the Age of Colorblindness*
Michael R. Gottfredson & Travis Hirschi's *A General Theory of Crime*
Richard Herrnstein & Charles A. Murray's *The Bell Curve: Intelligence and Class Structure in American Life*
Elizabeth Loftus's *Eyewitness Testimony*
Jay Macleod's *Ain't No Makin' It: Aspirations and Attainment in a Low-Income Neighborhood*
Philip Zimbardo's *The Lucifer Effect*

ECONOMICS

Janet Abu-Lughod's *Before European Hegemony*
Ha-Joon Chang's *Kicking Away the Ladder*
David Brion Davis's *The Problem of Slavery in the Age of Revolution*
Milton Friedman's *The Role of Monetary Policy*
Milton Friedman's *Capitalism and Freedom*
David Graeber's *Debt: the First 5000 Years*
Friedrich Hayek's *The Road to Serfdom*
Karen Ho's *Liquidated: An Ethnography of Wall Street*

The Macat Library By Discipline

John Maynard Keynes's *The General Theory of Employment, Interest and Money*
Charles P. Kindleberger's *Manias, Panics and Crashes*
Robert Lucas's *Why Doesn't Capital Flow from Rich to Poor Countries?*
Burton G. Malkiel's *A Random Walk Down Wall Street*
Thomas Robert Malthus's *An Essay on the Principle of Population*
Karl Marx's *Capital*
Thomas Piketty's *Capital in the Twenty-First Century*
Amartya Sen's *Development as Freedom*
Adam Smith's *The Wealth of Nations*
Nassim Nicholas Taleb's *The Black Swan: The Impact of the Highly Improbable*
Amos Tversky's & Daniel Kahneman's *Judgment under Uncertainty: Heuristics and Biases*
Mahbub Ul Haq's *Reflections on Human Development*
Max Weber's *The Protestant Ethic and the Spirit of Capitalism*

FEMINISM AND GENDER STUDIES

Judith Butler's *Gender Trouble*
Simone De Beauvoir's *The Second Sex*
Michel Foucault's *History of Sexuality*
Betty Friedan's *The Feminine Mystique*
Saba Mahmood's *The Politics of Piety: The Islamic Revival and the Feminist Subjec*t
Joan Wallach Scott's *Gender and the Politics of History*
Mary Wollstonecraft's *A Vindication of the Rights of Woman*
Virginia Woolf's *A Room of One's Own*

GEOGRAPHY

The Brundtland Report's *Our Common Future*
Rachel Carson's *Silent Spring*
Charles Darwin's *On the Origin of Species*
James Ferguson's *The Anti-Politics Machine*
Jane Jacobs's *The Death and Life of Great American Cities*
James Lovelock's *Gaia: A New Look at Life on Earth*
Amartya Sen's *Development as Freedom*
Mathis Wackernagel & William Rees's *Our Ecological Footprint*

HISTORY

Janet Abu-Lughod's *Before European Hegemony*
Benedict Anderson's *Imagined Communities*
Bernard Bailyn's *The Ideological Origins of the American Revolution*
Hanna Batatu's *The Old Social Classes And The Revolutionary Movements Of Iraq*
Christopher Browning's *Ordinary Men: Reserve Police Batallion 101 and the Final Solution in Poland*
Edmund Burke's *Reflections on the Revolution in France*
William Cronon's *Nature's Metropolis: Chicago And The Great West*
Alfred W. Crosby's *The Columbian Exchange*
Hamid Dabashi's *Iran: A People Interrupted*
David Brion Davis's *The Problem of Slavery in the Age of Revolution*
Nathalie Zemon Davis's *The Return of Martin Guerre*
Jared Diamond's *Guns, Germs & Steel: the Fate of Human Societies*
Frank Dikotter's *Mao's Great Famine*
John W Dower's *War Without Mercy: Race And Power In The Pacific War*
W. E. B. Du Bois's *The Souls of Black Folk*
Richard J. Evans's *In Defence of History*
Lucien Febvre's *The Problem of Unbelief in the 16th Century*
Sheila Fitzpatrick's *Everyday Stalinism*

Eric Foner's *Reconstruction: America's Unfinished Revolution, 1863-1877*
Michel Foucault's *Discipline and Punish*
Michel Foucault's *History of Sexuality*
Francis Fukuyama's *The End of History and the Last Man*
John Lewis Gaddis's *We Now Know: Rethinking Cold War History*
Ernest Gellner's *Nations and Nationalism*
Eugene Genovese's *Roll, Jordan, Roll: The World the Slaves Made*
Carlo Ginzburg's *The Night Battles*
Daniel Goldhagen's *Hitler's Willing Executioners*
Jack Goldstone's *Revolution and Rebellion in the Early Modern World*
Antonio Gramsci's *The Prison Notebooks*
Alexander Hamilton, John Jay & James Madison's *The Federalist Papers*
Christopher Hill's *The World Turned Upside Down*
Carole Hillenbrand's *The Crusades: Islamic Perspectives*
Thomas Hobbes's *Leviathan*
Eric Hobsbawm's *The Age Of Revolution*
John A. Hobson's *Imperialism: A Study*
Albert Hourani's *History of the Arab Peoples*
Samuel P. Huntington's *The Clash of Civilizations and the Remaking of World Order*
C. L. R. James's *The Black Jacobins*
Tony Judt's *Postwar: A History of Europe Since 1945*
Ernst Kantorowicz's *The King's Two Bodies: A Study in Medieval Political Theology*
Paul Kennedy's *The Rise and Fall of the Great Powers*
Ian Kershaw's *The "Hitler Myth": Image and Reality in the Third Reich*
John Maynard Keynes's *The General Theory of Employment, Interest and Money*
Charles P. Kindleberger's *Manias, Panics and Crashes*
Martin Luther King Jr's *Why We Can't Wait*
Henry Kissinger's *World Order: Reflections on the Character of Nations and the Course of History*
Thomas Kuhn's *The Structure of Scientific Revolutions*
Georges Lefebvre's *The Coming of the French Revolution*
John Locke's *Two Treatises of Government*
Niccolò Machiavelli's *The Prince*
Thomas Robert Malthus's *An Essay on the Principle of Population*
Mahmood Mamdani's *Citizen and Subject: Contemporary Africa And The Legacy Of Late Colonialism*
Karl Marx's *Capital*
Stanley Milgram's *Obedience to Authority*
John Stuart Mill's *On Liberty*
Thomas Paine's *Common Sense*
Thomas Paine's *Rights of Man*
Geoffrey Parker's *Global Crisis: War, Climate Change and Catastrophe in the Seventeenth Century*
Jonathan Riley-Smith's *The First Crusade and the Idea of Crusading*
Jean-Jacques Rousseau's *The Social Contract*
Joan Wallach Scott's *Gender and the Politics of History*
Theda Skocpol's *States and Social Revolutions*
Adam Smith's *The Wealth of Nations*
Timothy Snyder's *Bloodlands: Europe Between Hitler and Stalin*
Sun Tzu's *The Art of War*
Keith Thomas's *Religion and the Decline of Magic*
Thucydides's *The History of the Peloponnesian War*
Frederick Jackson Turner's *The Significance of the Frontier in American History*
Odd Arne Westad's *The Global Cold War: Third World Interventions And The Making Of Our Times*

LITERATURE

Chinua Achebe's *An Image of Africa: Racism in Conrad's Heart of Darkness*
Roland Barthes's *Mythologies*
Homi K. Bhabha's *The Location of Culture*
Judith Butler's *Gender Trouble*
Simone De Beauvoir's *The Second Sex*
Ferdinand De Saussure's *Course in General Linguistics*
T. S. Eliot's *The Sacred Wood: Essays on Poetry and Criticism*
Zora Neale Huston's *Characteristics of Negro Expression*
Toni Morrison's *Playing in the Dark: Whiteness in the American Literary Imagination*
Edward Said's *Orientalism*
Gayatri Chakravorty Spivak's *Can the Subaltern Speak?*
Mary Wollstonecraft's *A Vindication of the Rights of Women*
Virginia Woolf's *A Room of One's Own*

PHILOSOPHY

Elizabeth Anscombe's *Modern Moral Philosophy*
Hannah Arendt's *The Human Condition*
Aristotle's *Metaphysics*
Aristotle's *Nicomachean Ethics*
Edmund Gettier's *Is Justified True Belief Knowledge?*
Georg Wilhelm Friedrich Hegel's *Phenomenology of Spirit*
David Hume's *Dialogues Concerning Natural Religion*
David Hume's *The Enquiry for Human Understanding*
Immanuel Kant's *Religion within the Boundaries of Mere Reason*
Immanuel Kant's *Critique of Pure Reason*
Søren Kierkegaard's *The Sickness Unto Death*
Søren Kierkegaard's *Fear and Trembling*
C. S. Lewis's *The Abolition of Man*
Alasdair MacIntyre's *After Virtue*
Marcus Aurelius's *Meditations*
Friedrich Nietzsche's *On the Genealogy of Morality*
Friedrich Nietzsche's *Beyond Good and Evil*
Plato's *Republic*
Plato's *Symposium*
Jean-Jacques Rousseau's *The Social Contract*
Gilbert Ryle's *The Concept of Mind*
Baruch Spinoza's *Ethics*
Sun Tzu's *The Art of War*
Ludwig Wittgenstein's *Philosophical Investigations*

POLITICS

Benedict Anderson's *Imagined Communities*
Aristotle's *Politics*
Bernard Bailyn's *The Ideological Origins of the American Revolution*
Edmund Burke's *Reflections on the Revolution in France*
John C. Calhoun's *A Disquisition on Government*
Ha-Joon Chang's *Kicking Away the Ladder*
Hamid Dabashi's *Iran: A People Interrupted*
Hamid Dabashi's *Theology of Discontent: The Ideological Foundation of the Islamic Revolution in Iran*
Robert Dahl's *Democracy and its Critics*
Robert Dahl's *Who Governs?*
David Brion Davis's *The Problem of Slavery in the Age of Revolution*

Alexis De Tocqueville's *Democracy in America*
James Ferguson's *The Anti-Politics Machine*
Frank Dikotter's *Mao's Great Famine*
Sheila Fitzpatrick's *Everyday Stalinism*
Eric Foner's *Reconstruction: America's Unfinished Revolution, 1863-1877*
Milton Friedman's *Capitalism and Freedom*
Francis Fukuyama's *The End of History and the Last Man*
John Lewis Gaddis's *We Now Know: Rethinking Cold War History*
Ernest Gellner's *Nations and Nationalism*
David Graeber's *Debt: the First 5000 Years*
Antonio Gramsci's *The Prison Notebooks*
Alexander Hamilton, John Jay & James Madison's *The Federalist Papers*
Friedrich Hayek's *The Road to Serfdom*
Christopher Hill's *The World Turned Upside Down*
Thomas Hobbes's *Leviathan*
John A. Hobson's *Imperialism: A Study*
Samuel P. Huntington's *The Clash of Civilizations and the Remaking of World Order*
Tony Judt's *Postwar: A History of Europe Since 1945*
David C. Kang's *China Rising: Peace, Power and Order in East Asia*
Paul Kennedy's *The Rise and Fall of Great Powers*
Robert Keohane's *After Hegemony*
Martin Luther King Jr.'s *Why We Can't Wait*
Henry Kissinger's *World Order: Reflections on the Character of Nations and the Course of History*
John Locke's *Two Treatises of Government*
Niccolò Machiavelli's *The Prince*
Thomas Robert Malthus's *An Essay on the Principle of Population*
Mahmood Mamdani's *Citizen and Subject: Contemporary Africa And The Legacy Of Late Colonialism*
Karl Marx's *Capital*
John Stuart Mill's *On Liberty*
John Stuart Mill's *Utilitarianism*
Hans Morgenthau's *Politics Among Nations*
Thomas Paine's *Common Sense*
Thomas Paine's *Rights of Man*
Thomas Piketty's *Capital in the Twenty-First Century*
Robert D. Putman's *Bowling Alone*
John Rawls's *Theory of Justice*
Jean-Jacques Rousseau's *The Social Contract*
Theda Skocpol's *States and Social Revolutions*
Adam Smith's *The Wealth of Nations*
Sun Tzu's *The Art of War*
Henry David Thoreau's *Civil Disobedience*
Thucydides's *The History of the Peloponnesian War*
Kenneth Waltz's *Theory of International Politics*
Max Weber's *Politics as a Vocation*
Odd Arne Westad's *The Global Cold War: Third World Interventions And The Making Of Our Times*

POSTCOLONIAL STUDIES

Roland Barthes's *Mythologies*
Frantz Fanon's *Black Skin, White Masks*
Homi K. Bhabha's *The Location of Culture*
Gustavo Gutiérrez's *A Theology of Liberation*
Edward Said's *Orientalism*
Gayatri Chakravorty Spivak's *Can the Subaltern Speak?*

The Macat Library By Discipline

PSYCHOLOGY

Gordon Allport's *The Nature of Prejudice*
Alan Baddeley & Graham Hitch's *Aggression: A Social Learning Analysis*
Albert Bandura's *Aggression: A Social Learning Analysis*
Leon Festinger's *A Theory of Cognitive Dissonance*
Sigmund Freud's *The Interpretation of Dreams*
Betty Friedan's *The Feminine Mystique*
Michael R. Gottfredson & Travis Hirschi's *A General Theory of Crime*
Eric Hoffer's *The True Believer: Thoughts on the Nature of Mass Movements*
William James's *Principles of Psychology*
Elizabeth Loftus's *Eyewitness Testimony*
A. H. Maslow's *A Theory of Human Motivation*
Stanley Milgram's *Obedience to Authority*
Steven Pinker's *The Better Angels of Our Nature*
Oliver Sacks's *The Man Who Mistook His Wife For a Hat*
Richard Thaler & Cass Sunstein's *Nudge: Improving Decisions About Health, Wealth and Happiness*
Amos Tversky's *Judgment under Uncertainty: Heuristics and Biases*
Philip Zimbardo's *The Lucifer Effect*

SCIENCE

Rachel Carson's *Silent Spring*
William Cronon's *Nature's Metropolis: Chicago And The Great West*
Alfred W. Crosby's *The Columbian Exchange*
Charles Darwin's *On the Origin of Species*
Richard Dawkin's *The Selfish Gene*
Thomas Kuhn's *The Structure of Scientific Revolutions*
Geoffrey Parker's *Global Crisis: War, Climate Change and Catastrophe in the Seventeenth Century*
Mathis Wackernagel & William Rees's *Our Ecological Footprint*

SOCIOLOGY

Michelle Alexander's *The New Jim Crow: Mass Incarceration in the Age of Colorblindness*
Gordon Allport's *The Nature of Prejudice*
Albert Bandura's *Aggression: A Social Learning Analysis*
Hanna Batatu's *The Old Social Classes And The Revolutionary Movements Of Iraq*
Ha-Joon Chang's *Kicking Away the Ladder*
W. E. B. Du Bois's *The Souls of Black Folk*
Émile Durkheim's *On Suicide*
Frantz Fanon's *Black Skin, White Masks*
Frantz Fanon's *The Wretched of the Earth*
Eric Foner's *Reconstruction: America's Unfinished Revolution, 1863-1877*
Eugene Genovese's *Roll, Jordan, Roll: The World the Slaves Made*
Jack Goldstone's *Revolution and Rebellion in the Early Modern World*
Antonio Gramsci's *The Prison Notebooks*
Richard Herrnstein & Charles A Murray's *The Bell Curve: Intelligence and Class Structure in American Life*
Eric Hoffer's *The True Believer: Thoughts on the Nature of Mass Movements*
Jane Jacobs's *The Death and Life of Great American Cities*
Robert Lucas's *Why Doesn't Capital Flow from Rich to Poor Countries?*
Jay Macleod's *Ain't No Makin' It: Aspirations and Attainment in a Low Income Neighborhood*
Elaine May's *Homeward Bound: American Families in the Cold War Era*
Douglas McGregor's *The Human Side of Enterprise*
C. Wright Mills's *The Sociological Imagination*

Thomas Piketty's *Capital in the Twenty-First Century*
Robert D. Putman's *Bowling Alone*
David Riesman's *The Lonely Crowd: A Study of the Changing American Character*
Edward Said's *Orientalism*
Joan Wallach Scott's *Gender and the Politics of History*
Theda Skocpol's *States and Social Revolutions*
Max Weber's *The Protestant Ethic and the Spirit of Capitalism*

THEOLOGY

Augustine's *Confessions*
Benedict's *Rule of St Benedict*
Gustavo Gutiérrez's *A Theology of Liberation*
Carole Hillenbrand's *The Crusades: Islamic Perspectives*
David Hume's *Dialogues Concerning Natural Religion*
Immanuel Kant's *Religion within the Boundaries of Mere Reason*
Ernst Kantorowicz's *The King's Two Bodies: A Study in Medieval Political Theology*
Søren Kierkegaard's *The Sickness Unto Death*
C. S. Lewis's *The Abolition of Man*
Saba Mahmood's *The Politics of Piety: The Islamic Revival and the Feminist Subjec*t
Baruch Spinoza's *Ethics*
Keith Thomas's *Religion and the Decline of Magic*

COMING SOON

Chris Argyris's *The Individual and the Organisation*
Seyla Benhabib's *The Rights of Others*
Walter Benjamin's *The Work Of Art in the Age of Mechanical Reproduction*
John Berger's *Ways of Seeing*
Pierre Bourdieu's *Outline of a Theory of Practice*
Mary Douglas's *Purity and Danger*
Roland Dworkin's *Taking Rights Seriously*
James G. March's *Exploration and Exploitation in Organisational Learning*
Ikujiro Nonaka's *A Dynamic Theory of Organizational Knowledge Creation*
Griselda Pollock's *Vision and Difference*
Amartya Sen's *Inequality Re-Examined*
Susan Sontag's *On Photography*
Yasser Tabbaa's *The Transformation of Islamic Art*
Ludwig von Mises's *Theory of Money and Credit*

Macat Disciplines

Access the greatest ideas and thinkers across entire disciplines, including

AFRICANA STUDIES

Chinua Achebe's *An Image of Africa: Racism in Conrad's Heart of Darkness*

W. E. B. Du Bois's *The Souls of Black Folk*

Zora Neale Hurston's *Characteristics of Negro Expression*

Martin Luther King Jr.'s *Why We Can't Wait*

Toni Morrison's *Playing in the Dark: Whiteness in the American Literary Imagination*

Macat analyses are available from all good bookshops and libraries.

Access hundreds of analyses through one, multimedia tool.
Join free for one month **library.macat.com**

Macat Disciplines

Access the greatest ideas and thinkers across entire disciplines, including

FEMINISM, GENDER AND QUEER STUDIES

Simone De Beauvoir's
The Second Sex

Michel Foucault's
History of Sexuality

Betty Friedan's
The Feminine Mystique

Saba Mahmood's
*The Politics of Piety:
The Islamic Revival and
the Feminist Subject*

Joan Wallach Scott's
*Gender and the
Politics of History*

Mary Wollstonecraft's
*A Vindication of the
Rights of Woman*

Virginia Woolf's
A Room of One's Own

Judith Butler's
Gender Trouble

Macat analyses are available from all good bookshops and libraries.

Access hundreds of analyses through one, multimedia tool.
Join free for one month **library.macat.com**

Macat Disciplines

Access the greatest ideas and thinkers across entire disciplines, including

INEQUALITY

Ha-Joon Chang's, *Kicking Away the Ladder*

David Graeber's, *Debt: The First 5000 Years*

Robert E. Lucas's, *Why Doesn't Capital Flow from Rich To Poor Countries?*

Thomas Piketty's, *Capital in the Twenty-First Century*

Amartya Sen's, *Inequality Re-Examined*

Mahbub Ul Haq's, *Reflections on Human Development*

Macat analyses are available from all good bookshops and libraries.

Access hundreds of analyses through one, multimedia tool.
Join free for one month **library.macat.com**

Macat Disciplines

Access the greatest ideas and thinkers across entire disciplines, including

CRIMINOLOGY

Michelle Alexander's
*The New Jim Crow:
Mass Incarceration in the
Age of Colorblindness*

**Michael R. Gottfredson
& Travis Hirschi's**
A General Theory of Crime

Elizabeth Loftus's
Eyewitness Testimony

**Richard Herrnstein
& Charles A. Murray's**
*The Bell Curve: Intelligence and
Class Structure in American Life*

Jay Macleod's
*Ain't No Makin' It:
Aspirations and Attainment in a
Low-Income Neighborhood*

Philip Zimbardo's
The Lucifer Effect

Macat analyses are available from all good bookshops and libraries.

Access hundreds of analyses through one, multimedia tool.
Join free for one month **library.macat.com**

Macat Disciplines

Access the greatest ideas and thinkers across entire disciplines, including

Postcolonial Studies

Roland Barthes's *Mythologies*
Frantz Fanon's *Black Skin, White Masks*
Homi K. Bhabha's *The Location of Culture*
Gustavo Gutiérrez's *A Theology of Liberation*
Edward Said's *Orientalism*
Gayatri Chakravorty Spivak's *Can the Subaltern Speak?*

Macat Disciplines

Access the greatest ideas and thinkers across entire disciplines, including

GLOBALIZATION

Arjun Appadurai's, *Modernity at Large: Cultural Dimensions of Globalisation*

James Ferguson's, *The Anti-Politics Machine*

Geert Hofstede's, *Culture's Consequences*

Amartya Sen's, *Development as Freedom*

Macat Pairs

Analyse historical and modern issues from opposite sides of an argument. Pairs include:

HOW TO RUN AN ECONOMY

John Maynard Keynes's
The General Theory OF Employment, Interest and Money

Classical economics suggests that market economies are self-correcting in times of recession or depression, and tend toward full employment and output. But English economist John Maynard Keynes disagrees.

In his ground-breaking 1936 study *The General Theory*, Keynes argues that traditional economics has misunderstood the causes of unemployment. Employment is not determined by the price of labor; it is directly linked to demand. Keynes believes market economies are by nature unstable, and so require government intervention. Spurred on by the social catastrophe of the Great Depression of the 1930s, he sets out to revolutionize the way the world thinks

Milton Friedman's
The Role of Monetary Policy

Friedman's 1968 paper changed the course of economic theory. In just 17 pages, he demolished existing theory and outlined an effective alternate monetary policy designed to secure 'high employment, stable prices and rapid growth.'

Friedman demonstrated that monetary policy plays a vital role in broader economic stability and argued that economists got their monetary policy wrong in the 1950s and 1960s by misunderstanding the relationship between inflation and unemployment. Previous generations of economists had believed that governments could permanently decrease unemployment by permitting inflation—and vice versa. Friedman's most original contribution was to show that this supposed trade-off is an illusion that only works in the short term.

Macat Disciplines

*Access the greatest ideas and thinkers
across entire disciplines, including*

THE FUTURE OF DEMOCRACY

Robert A. Dahl's, *Democracy and Its Critics*
Robert A. Dahl's, *Who Governs?*
Alexis De Toqueville's, *Democracy in America*
Niccolò Machiavelli's, *The Prince*
John Stuart Mill's, *On Liberty*
Robert D. Putnam's, *Bowling Alone*
Jean-Jacques Rousseau's, *The Social Contract*
Henry David Thoreau's, *Civil Disobedience*

For Product Safety Concerns and Information please contact our EU
representative GPSR@taylorandfrancis.com Taylor & Francis Verlag GmbH,
Kaufingerstraße 24, 80331 München, Germany

Printed and bound by CPI Group (UK) Ltd, Croydon, CR0 4YY
08/06/2025
01896977-0008